GUIDELINES FOR COLLECTION DEVELOPMENT

David L. Perkins, editor

Collection Development Committee,
Resources and Technical Services Division,
American Library Association

AMERICAN LIBRARY ASSOCIATION
Chicago

Library of Congress Cataloging in Publication Data

American Library Association. Collection Development
  Committee.
  Guidelines for collection development.

    Bibliography: p.
    1. Collection development (Libraries). I. Perkins,
David, 1939-   II. Title.
Z687.A518 1979   025.2   79-16971
ISBN 0-8389-3231-2

Printed in the United States of America
Third printing, March 1981

Contents

Preface

The Collection Development Committee of the Resources Section, Resources and Technical Services Division, American Library Association, was organized to provide a focus in ALA for activities relating to collection development, and, in particular, to: study the present resources of American libraries and the coordination of collection development programs; develop guidelines for the definition of selection policies; evaluate and recommend selection tools for collection development; and recommend qualifications and requisite training for selection personnel. In partial response to these charges, the Committee at its New York meeting of 9 July 1974 appointed task forces comprised of committee members and consultants to prepare guidelines for the following collection development activities: formula budgeting and allocation; the formulation of collection development policies; the development of review programs designed to assist in the solution of space problems; and the description and evaluation of library collections. The guidelines presented here are the result of the work of these task groups. The format and numbering system used in these guidelines have been taken from the American Library Association's Committee on Standards' *ALA Standards Manual* (1976).

Thomas Shaughnessy, Hans Weber, and Sheila Dowd (Chair) prepared *Guidelines for the Formulation of Collection Development Policies.* The *Guidelines* were submitted to the Committee for revision at its meetings of January and July 1975; they were further revised at the Committee's meeting of 19 January 1976 when they were approved for submission to the Executive Committee of the Resources Section. A "preliminary edition," dated March 1976, was approved by the Executive Committee on 19 July 1976 and approved by the Board of Directors of RTSD by a mail ballot in August 1976. The preliminary *Guidelines* appeared in the winter 1977 issue of *Library Resources and Technical*

Services (vol. 21, no. 1, pp. 40–46). The version of the *Guidelines* appearing herein is a revision of the *LRTS* draft, which was approved by the RTSD Board of Directors by a mail ballot during the fall of 1978.

Task force members George B. Miller, Jr. (Chair) and Robert W. Butler, with George S. Bonn and Paul Mosher as consultants, prepared *Guidelines for the Evaluation of the Effectiveness of Library Collections.*

Guidelines for the Review of Library Collections was prepared by a task force initially consisting of David Zubatsky and David Perkins and subsequently revised by David Perkins and Paul Mosher. After their approval by the Collection Development Committee, and by the Resources Section Board, both *Guidelines for the Evaluation of the Effectivensss of Library Collections* and *Guidelines for the Review of Library Collections* were approved by the RTSD Board of Directors by a mail ballot during the fall of 1978.

Jean Coberly; Jean Boyer Hamlin; and Elaine Sloan, consultant, wrote *Guidelines for the Allocation of Library Materials Budgets.* This was approved by the Collection Development Committee and the Resources Section Board during the fall of 1978 by mail ballots and by the RTSD Board of Directors at the 1979 Midwinter meeting.

The bibliography on Collection Development Policies was compiled by the 1978 Program-organizing Committee of the Southern California Chapter of the Collection Development Librarian's Chapter of the California Library Association. This bibliography was attached because it lists and annotates important sources. The other bibliographies were compiled by the task groups who drafted guidelines, and the sources listed constituted important elements in the process of guideline formulation.

Guidelines for the Formulation of Collection Development Policies

1. INTRODUCTION

1.1   Purpose.

The Committee offers these *Guidelines for the Formulation of Collection Development Policies* in the belief that collection development policy statements must be comprehensible and comparable if they are to prove useful in the implementation of long-range goals for sharing of resources. To promote comprehensibility and comparability, policy statements must employ language which is clearly defined, and measures whose values are commonly understood.

1.2   Objectives.

The immediate aims of the designers of these *Guidelines* are to identify the essential elements of a written statement of collection development policy, and to establish a standard terminology and structure for use in the preparation of such policies.

1.3   Need.

Widespread budgetary constraints and the growth of interlibrary cooperation for shared resources and service networks have given impetus to the pressure to analyze collection activity in universally comprehensible terms.

1.4   Scope.

The Committee has attempted to provide an instrument that will be of use to libraries of all kinds and sizes in formulating statements of their collection development policies. All elements of the *Guidelines*, however, will not be equally applicable to all libraries.

1.5   Audience.

The *Guidelines* are intended to help library administrators and collection development librarians to produce a document that can serve as both a planning tool and a communications device. The resulting policy statements should clarify collection development objectives to staff, users, and cooperating institutions, enabling them to identify areas of strength in library collections; and by this means should facilitate the coordination of collection development and cooperative services within an area or region. The policy statement can itself serve as a communication to some audiences. For other selected audiences, among them library users, funding authorities, and governing boards, the statement should be reviewed as the data file from which interpretative statements can be formulated.

1.6   Methodology.

The *Guidelines* have been submitted to the Committee in open meeting at several Midwinter and Annual Conferences. The group discussions, in which numerous visitors have participated, have resulted in extensive revisions of the initial drafts.

1.7   Assumptions.

1.7.1   A written collection development policy statement is for any library a desirable tool, which: (a) enables selectors to work with greater consistency toward defined goals, thus shaping stronger collections and using funds more wisely; (b) informs library staff, users, administrators, trustees, and others as to the scope and nature of existing collections, and the plans for continuing development of resources; (c) provides information which will assist in the budgetary allocation process.

1.7.2   A library's policy for deselection (that is, identification of works which may be removed to remote storage locations or discarded) should be coordinated with its collection development policy. (See below *Guidelines for the Review of Library Collections*.)

1.7.3   It is desirable that form and terminology of collection development policy statements be sufficiently standardized to permit comparison between institutions.

1.7.4   Libraries have acknowledged the impossibility of building totally comprehensive collections, and will increasingly need to rely on cooperative activities. Collection development policy statements will assist cooperative collection building, and will also be of value to users and user-service units in locating materials.

1.8　　　　Definitions.

1.8.1　　　Levels of collection density and collecting intensity.

1.8.1.1　　Assumptions.

Definitions of collecting levels are not to be applied in a relative or *ad hoc* manner (that is, relative to a given library or group of libraries), but in a very objective manner. Consequently, it is quite likely that a large number of libraries will not hold comprehensive collections in any area. Similarly, academic libraries that do not support doctoral programs, or other types of libraries that are not oriented toward special research, may not have any collections that would fall within the research level as defined herein. The definitions are proposed to describe a range and diversity of titles and forms of materials; they do not address the question of availability of multiple copies of the same title.

1.8.1.2　　Codes.

The codes defined below are designed for use in identifying both the extent of existing collections in given subject fields (collection density) and the extent of current collecting acitivity in the field (collecting intensity).

A. Comprehensive level. A collection in which a library endeavors, so far as is reasonably possible, to include all significant works of recorded knowledge (publications, manuscripts, other forms) for a necessarily defined field. This level of collecting intensity is that which maintains a "special collection"; the aim, if not the achievement, is exhaustiveness.

B. Research level. A collection which includes the major published source materials required for dissertations and independent research, including materials containing research reporting, new findings, scientific experimental results, and other information useful to researchers. It also includes all important reference works and a wide selection of specialized monographs, as well as an extensive collection of journals and major indexing and abstracting services in the field.

C. Study level. A collection which supports undergraduate or graduate course work, or sustained independent study; that is, which is adequate to maintain knowledge of a subject required for limited or generalized purposes, of less than research intensity. It includes a wide range of basic monographs, complete collections of the works of important writers, selections from the works of secondary writers, a selection of representative journals, and the reference tools and fundamental bibliographical apparatus pertaining to the subject.

NOTE: Some college librarians have expressed a need for further refinement of the "Study level" code for use by libraries without comprehensive or research level collections, to enable them to define their collecting policies explicitly enough to meet the needs of network resources planning. We include the following optional subcodes for such institutions.

(1) Advanced study level. A collection which is adequate to support the course work of advanced undergraduate and master's degree programs, or sustained independent study; that is, which is adequate to maintain knowledge of a subject required for limited or generalized purposes, of less than research intensity. It includes a wide range of basic monographs both current and retrospective, complete collections of the works of more important writers, selections from the works of secondary writers, a selection of representative journals, and the reference tools and fundamental bibliographical apparatus pertaining to the subject.

(2) Initial study level. A collection which is adequate to support undergraduate courses. It includes a judicious selection from currently published basic monographs (as are represented by *Choice* selections) supported by seminal retrospective monographs (as are represented by *Books for College Libraries*); a broad selection of works of more important writers; a selection of the most significant works of secondary writers; a selection of the major review journals; and current editions of the most significant reference tools and bibliographies pertaining to the subject.

D.   Basic level. A highly selective collection which serves to introduce and define the subject and to indicate the varieties of information available elsewhere. It includes major dictionaries and encyclopedias, selected editions of important works, historical surveys, important bibliographies, and a few major periodicals in the field.

E. Minimal level. A subject area in which few selections are made beyond very basic works.

NOTE: Some subject fields may be completely out of scope for a library's collections. These class numbers can be lined out in the analysis, or "0" can be used to indicate "not collected."

1.8.2   Language codes.

The following codes should be used to indicate languages in which material is collected. Libraries wishing a greater refinement of this data may subcode with the MARC language codes.

F. All applicable languages (i.e., no exclusions)
G. English
H. Romance languages
J. Germanic languages
K. Slavic languages
L. Middle Eastern languages
M. Asian languages
N. African languages
P. Other languages

2. GUIDELINES

2.1   Principles governing formulation and application of collection development policies.

2.1.1   Libraries should identify the long- and short-range needs of their clientele, and establish priorities for the allocation of resources to meet those needs. A collection development policy statement is an orderly expression of those priorities as they relate to the development of library resources.

2.1.2   Collection development policy statements should be reviewed at regular intervals to insure that changes in defined goals, user needs, and priorities are recognized, and that changing budgetary situations are confronted.

2.1.3   A library's collection development policy should be coordinated with those of appropriate other libraries, whether in a hierarchy of dependence, or in a division of responsibility among equals. A collection development policy statement should assist librarians to select and deselect in conformity with regional needs and resources.

2.2   Elements of a collection development policy statement.

2.2.1   Analysis of general institutional objectives.
             This section should include:
             A. Clientele to be served
             B. General subject boundaries of the collection
             C. Kinds of programs or user needs supported (research, instruc-
                 tional, recreational, general information, reference, etc.)
             D. General priorities and limitations governing selection, including:
                 (1) Degree of continuing support for strong collections
                 (2) Forms of material collected or excluded
                 (3) Languages, geographical areas collected or excluded
                 (4) Chronological periods collected or excluded
                 (5) Other exclusions
                 (6) Duplication of materials (generally treated)
                 NOTE: The collection development policy statement addresses
                 the question of breadth and depth of subject coverage. Libraries
                 will need to formulate separate statements of policy relating to
                 duplication of materials; and such additional policy statements
                 must be given consideration in fund allocation.
             E. Regional, national, or local cooperative collection agreements
                 which complement or otherwise affect the institutions policy
             F. Legal, regulatory, or policy requirements of the institution.

2.2.2   Detailed analysis of collection development policy for subject fields.
             It is recommended that this analysis be organized by classification
             scheme, with a parenthetical subject following the class number for
             ease of interpretation. The organization by class assures that the
             library's practice and policy with regard to the entire range of knowl-
             edge will be examined; and that the language used in the subject
             analysis will be as much as possible in a *lingua franca* for internal and
             interinstitutional discussions. Many libraries have chosen to design
             their collection development policy statements with an organization
             by academic program or broad subject descriptor. In such instances
             an index by class will facilitate cooperative resources planning with
             other libraries.

             Libraries will differ in the degree of detail they will require for the
             analysis of their collection development policy by class. A suggested
             minimum refinement of the Library of Congress classification on
             which to structure the analysis is the breakdown into approximately

five hundred subdivisions used in *Titles Classified by the Library of Congress Classification: National Shelflist Count, 1977*, Berkeley, General Library, Univ. of California, 1977 (see Appendix A). For Dewey or other classification schemes a comparably refined breakdown should be attempted. It must be stressed that this recommendation indicates a minimal refinement of classification analysis needed for interinstitutional comparisons. Many libraries will prefer to analyze their collections in greater detail.

For each subject category (i.e., classification number or group of numbers), indicate the following:

A.   Level of collecting intensity codes to indicate
    (1) Existing strength of collection
    (2) Actual current level of collection activity
    (3) Desirable level of collecting to meet program needs
B.   Languages
C.   Chronological periods collected
D.   Geographic areas collected
E.   Forms of material collection
F.   Library unit or selector with primary selection responsibility for the field.

2.2.3   Detailed analysis of collection development policy for form collections.

In some libraries special collection development policy statements are required for certain forms of materials, where policy governing the collection of those materials differs from the library's general policy for subject collections. Some examples of forms for which special policy statements may be needed include:

A.   Newspapers
B.   Microform collections
C.   Manuscripts
D.   Government publications
E.   Maps
F.   Audiovisual materials
G.   Data tapes.

Where possible, it is desirable that the basic structure of the policy statement for a form collection follow subject classification; but with some form collections it will be necessary to use another primary arrangement (kind of material, area, etc.). For example, the policy statement for a map collection might be divided first into "general maps," "topographic maps," "raised relief maps," etc., with subdivision by area classification; that for a newspaper collection might be primarily by political division.

Whatever the basic structure chosen, the detailed analysis of collection development for a form collection should include the elements identified in 2.2.3.A–F above.

2.2.4   Indexes.

The information in the policy statement should be made accessible for a wide variety of purposes. To this end an index should be appended which correlates subject terms to class numbers. Individual libraries may also wish to index by academic programs, library units, or other key words or concepts.

Guidelines for the Evaluation of the Effectiveness of Library Collections

1. INTRODUCTION

1.1   Purpose.

This document is intended to provide librarians and others with a statement of principles and methods to guide them in determining the extent to which their library actually did acquire the books, journals, or other materials it intended to acquire; in other words, whether the library's collection is fulfilling its purpose.

1.2   Objectives.

The immediate aims of these *Guidelines* are to identify the essential elements of the evaluation process and to list the advantages and disadvantages of each.

1.3   Need.

Every library collection should be established for a definite purpose. The collection may be developed for research, recreation, community service and development, instruction, support of a corporate activity, or a combination of these. In any case, evaluations should be made to determine whether the collection is meeting its objectives, how well it is serving its users, in which ways or areas it is deficient, and what remains to be done to develop the collection. These guidelines are needed to aid in making such an evaluation.

The library administrator should not simply assume that the collection satisfies the research, instructional, developmental, recreational, or corporate needs of the community of users. Rather, subjectivity

9

of judgment should be reduced as much as possible by the use of measurement techniques. Available methods for determining the value of a collection are not completely objective or free of interpretation by the evaluators, nor are they foolproof in their application and outcome. However, procedures are available which can reduce individual interpretation, if that seems advisable. If applied and administered carefully, or if used in combination with one another, the procedures can demonstrate with reasonable assurance how well a collection satisfies the purpose of the library as perceived at any one time. Techniques of measurement should be standardized when possible so that the results of evaluation of different collections might be comparable. Increasingly, libraries are finding that they cannot afford to develop their collections in all areas in which they might wish to do so; therefore, they are considering sharing of resources. If the collection of one library can be shown by reasonable and comparative measurements to be strong in an area or in several areas, another library or other libraries may decide not to be overly concerned about collecting in that area or those areas, perhaps negotiating a cooperative agreement on the use of collections.

1.4   Scope.

These *Guidelines* list various methods to be used in evaluating collections of libraries, indicating the types of library for which each method can be used and advantages and disadvantages of each method. The document is not intended to describe each method in detail, as this has already been done in the literature; it only sets forth a checklist to serve as a guide in considering the most appropriate method(s) of collection evaluation for a specific library or type of library.

1.5   Audience.

These *Guidelines* are intended for library administrators; for collection development officers; for those who adjust collection development (selection) policies as needed to fill in weak areas of the collection; for administrators considering cooperative agreement in the area of collection development; for accreditation boards; or for administrators of the university, corporation, high school, political jurisdiction or other body of which the library is a part.

1.6   Methodology.

Two literature searches were conducted: (1) a computer search of a large number of data bases, and (2) a standard manual search. The most valuable published source found was George S. Bonn's article "Evaluation of the Collection," *Library Trends,* 22 (3), January 1974, pages 265–304.

The summary of evaluation methods in these *Guidelines* reflects, to a large extent, those given in the Bonn article and, to a lesser extent, those given in the F. W. Lancaster book, *Measurement and Evaluation of Library Services,* Washington, Information Resources Press, 1977 (cf. section 2.2, measures). "Evaluation of the Collection" and "Evaluation of Document Delivery Capabilities" are the chapters that were used from that book in manuscript. Both of these publications and their extensive lists of references are strongly recommended for further information on collection evaluation. References to more complete discussions are included in the *Guidelines* only when the measure described is set forth basically in one paper.

Following our literature searches, guidelines were drafted and submitted to five successive meetings of the ALA/RTSD/RS Collection Development Committee for revisions. In addition, suggestions were elicited from participants of the ALA Preconference on Collection Development, Detroit, June 1977.

2. GUIDELINES

2.1   Statement of principles.

The value or worth of something is measured by determining how well it is satisfying its purpose. Its purpose, therefore, must be clearly agreed upon and set forth before any evaluation of a library's collection can take place.

The goals and purposes of the collection should be stated in a collection development (selection) policy. Since the development of the collection through selecting can be very subjective, a written policy about what is to be selected or rejected should be developed. Another set of guidelines by the Collection Development Committee sets forth the manner in which such a policy might be formulated and what it should contain. With some evaluation methods, the collection development policy should serve as the yardstick against which the evaluative measurements are made, for instance, when evaluating by searching lists which are chosen on the basis of their appropriateness as set forth in the collection development policy.

Some evaluative procedures might show where the policy needs to be changed, for instance, when evaluating the collection on the basis of what the library clientele is actually requesting or using.

Even with a written collection development policy, judgment is still required. In evaluation, judgment is involved more with some techniques than with those that attempt to quantify. Quantitative methods alone may not be completely satisfactory. The tension between the qualitative and quantitative cannot be fully resolved. The problem is: can the quality of something be measured with quantitative technique? Yet, if no quantitative procedures are involved in the assessment, there may be no basis of comparability with other libraries, less reliability because of the subjective nature of the method. Quantitative methods are more conducive to standardization and comparability, which allows some basis for rating library collections of a similar type for accreditation purposes, for meeting standards, for deciding on sharing of collections, or simply for knowing how one library stands in relation to other libraries.

The presentation of methods which follows is intended to provide sufficient guidance for the evaluator to choose an appropriate method or combination of methods to suit his or her purpose and to make a reasonably reliable evaluation. Some methods may be used in combination with other methods. Often it is advisable to use both quantitative and qualitative techniques. The listings which follow are illustrative rather than exhaustive.

2.2   Measures.

2.2.1   Checking lists, catalogs, bibliographies.

With this procedure the evaluator uses lists of titles or works appropriate to the subjects collected or programs of the library. These lists are then searched in the library files to determine the percentage the library has in its own collection. Presumably a high percentage of items found indicates successful collection development.

Types of lists are:

A. Standard catalogs and basic general lists, such as ALA's basic collections, *Books for College Libraries, Choice's Opening Day Collection*
B. Printed catalogs of the holdings of important and specialized libraries
C. Specialized bibliographies and basic lists

    D. Current lists, such as bestseller lists, books of selected publishers, annual subject compilations

    E. Lists of reference works

    F. Lists of periodicals

    G. Authorized lists prepared by governmental authorities or professional associations

    H. *Ad hoc* lists compiled for a specific library or type of library or for purposes of matching a certain objective

    I. Citations contained in publications, such as footnotes, bibliographies, references

    J. Lists of most frequently cited journals

    K. Lists, usually in up-to-date journals, of evaluated publications at the forefront of current research

    L. Dealers'/publishers'/auction catalogs

    M. Course syllabi or reading lists

    N. Bibliographies in faculty or staff members' theses or dissertations.

The type of list used to check the collection depends on the type of collection being checked and the purposes of the evaluation. For example, a "basic" collection in an undergraduate library may be checked against "standard" lists developed for this type of collection. The list must match the objectives and type of collection a library has.

2.2.1.1   Advantages.

    A. A variety of published lists is available: comprehensive, specialized, general, popular, or research.

    B. Many available lists are backed by the authority and competence of expert librarians or subject specialists.

    C. Lists of current materials are generally available since many lists are updated regularly.

    D. Lists can be compiled according to the needs of an individual library or type of library.

    E. The procedure of searching lists is easy to apply.

2.2.1.2   Disadvantages.

    A. Available lists may have been used previously as buying guides by the library being evaluated.

    B. Lists representing the viewpoint of one individual or group may not represent the subject well.

    C. Lists even in appropriate subjects may not reflect the interests or purposes of a library.

D. Many lists are not revised and become out-of-date.
E. Lists may not be as representative of the library's subjects or purposes as its holdings are.
F. In some areas lists may be hard to find or compile.

2.2.2   Examining the collection directly.

By this procedure someone, presumably a person familiar with the literature of a subject(s), physically looks over the materials on the shelf. The examination may reveal size, scope, depth, and significance of the collection; recency of material; and physical condition. Furthermore, preservation, conservation, restoration, or replacement of materials may be taken into consideration in the process. For guidance in these matters see below the Collection Development Committee's *Guidelines for Review of Library Collections.*

2.2.2.1 Advantages.

A. This method can be accomplished quickly.
B. Strengths and weaknesses of the collection can be evaluated rapidly.
C. The method can be applied to any library collection.
D. Cooperative collecting policies can be developed by evaluating strong and weak collection areas of participating libraries.

2.2.2.2 Disadvantages.

A. Persons knowledgeable in a subject and its literature are required, and they may be difficult to locate.
B. This method is impressionistic and does not follow quantitative methods.
C. The materials may not be on the shelf. The shelf list should be used at the same time the shelves are being checked.

2.2.3   Compiling statistics.

By this method statistics of various kinds are collected:

A. Size:
      Number of volumes or titles in the library
      Number of periodical subscriptions
      Measurement of shelf list
      Number of volumes by date of publication.

B. Volumes added in a period of time:
      Measurement of additions to shelf list
      Relationship to circulation statistics

All measurements preferably by subject or class
Cataloging statistics.

C. Expenditures for library materials:
New books
New periodicals
Annual or longer time period
By subject classes
Percentage of total library budget
Amount per user or class of user.

D. Formulae:

Clapp-Jordan. For academic research libraries, measures core collection; volumes per student, per faculty, per graduate field, per undergraduate honors program.[1]

Cartter "library resources index." For research libraries, measures total volumes, volumes added annually, number of current periodicals.[2]

Beasley formula. For potential public library service, measure resources, population, circulation, research capability.[3]

Voigt formula. For university libraries, provides a method for determining an adequate annual acquisition rate of current materials for a university; acquisition rate for graduate fields, for undergraduate students, for research programs as affected by access to other research libraries.[4]

E. Circulation statistics:
For different classes of users
For different subject classes of books
By date of material

[1] Verner W. Clapp and Robert T. Jordan, "Quantitative Criteria for Adequacy of Academic Library Collections," *College and Research Libraries* 26(5):371–80 (Sept. 1965).

[2] Alan M. Cartter, *An Assessment of Quality in Graduate Education* (Washington, D. C.: American Council on Education, 1966), p. 114–15.

[3] Kenneth E. Beasley, "A Theoretical Framework for Public Library Measurement," in *Research Methods in Librarianship: Measurement and Evaluation,* ed. by Herbert Goldhor (Urbana: Univ. of Illinois Graduate School of the Library Sciences, 1968), p. 2–14.

[4] Melvin J. Voigt, "Acquisition Rates in University Libraries," *College and Research Libraries* 36(4):263–71 (July 1975).

By type of format of material

At different times of the year

Compared with acquisition statistics, preferably by subject or class.

F. Unfilled requests and filled requests:

By subject class, i.e., books or journals

By form of material

Compared with acquisition statistics, preferably by subject or class.

G. Interlibrary loan requests: how many requests from a library's clientele must go outside?

By subject class

By different classes of users

By form of material.

Consider cooperative arrangements.

H. Optimum size. Core collection of books or journals most likely to be used:

Journal-use statistics and Bradford-Zipf distribution[5]

Circulation records of books.

2.2.3.1   Advantages.

A. Some records of statistics may be easily kept.

B. If proper records have been kept, they are easily available.

C. If clearly defined, they may be widely understood and comparable.

D. Formulas take into account multiple factors affecting collection size or growth.

E. Circulation statistics; requests filled and unfilled and interlibrary loan requests relate directly to the collections' users.

2.2.3.2   Disadvantages.

A. Statistics may be recorded improperly.

B. Clear definitions of units may be lacking.

C. Statistical records may not be comparable.

D. Significance of statistics may be difficult to interpret.

E. Involved formulas may not be applied consistently and comparably, e.g., in supplying figures and weighting.

[5]B. C. Brookes, "The Derivation and Application of the Bradford-Zipf Distribution," *Journal of Documentation* 24(4):247–65 (Dec. 1968).

2.2.4   Citations from papers of library users.

This method is most useful for university, special, or other libraries with clearly identified groups of users. It consists of determining the holdings of items cited in footnotes, bibliographies, or references of papers; articles or books written by faculty, research staff, or others writing in areas covered by the library's collection. It is assumed that the writer has found it necessary or desirable to use sources outside the library which serves him or her.

2.2.4.1   Advantages.
   A.   Lists are easy to come by.
   B.   They are tailor-made by the library clientele.
   C.   The procedure can be easily applied.
   D.   The method relates directly to the interest of the users.
   E.   The lists will apply to peripherally related materials of the general collection required by scholars.
   F.   The procedure allows for changing interests.

2.2.4.2   Disadvantages.
   A.   The author may have limited himself or herself to use of the library being evaluated. Collection bias may also be a problem.
   B.   The citations may relate to a limited area of the collection.
   C.   Some peripheral areas may be out of scope.
   D.   The method is limited to a user group which writes papers.

2.2.5   User opinions.

This procedure requires a survey of users or user groups, obtaining verbal or written responses in interviews or questionnaires or both.

2.2.5.1   Advantages.
   A.   The survey relates directly to the needs of users, and thus to the goals or objectives of the library.
   B.   It reflects changing interests and trends.
   C.   It can be done for most types of clientele.

2.2.5.2   Disadvantages.
   A.   This method requires active solicitation of opinions.
   B.   Users are often subjective, inconsistent, uninformed, or passive.
   C.   User interests may be focused more narrowly than collection development policies.

2.2.6   Application of standards.

This procedure can be used by those types of libraries for which standards have been developed. Standards are available for many types of libraries.

2.2.6.1   Advantages.

A. For the appropriate type of library the standard will generally relate closely to the library goals.
B. Standards are generally widely accepted and authoritative.
C. They may be promulgated and used for evaluation by accrediting agencies.
D. They may be very persuasive in engendering support for the library.

2.2.6.2   Disadvantages.

A. Many are stated generally and difficult to apply.
B. They may require a high degree of professional knowledge and judgment.
C. Knowledgeable people may disagree in application or results.
D. Minimum standards may be regarded as maximum standards.

2.2.7   Total resources and document delivery tests.

Increasingly, libraries are becoming interdependent. One library cannot meet all the needs of all its users. Therefore, cooperative systems have developed wherein the use of other libraries may not indicate a collection development problem, but rather an intended result of cooperation and sharing of resources. If the cooperative system fills all requests on a timely basis, regardless of where in the system the material came from, its purpose is accomplished. Statistical methods have been developed for surveys measuring a library's capability of supplying documents. A measure of document delivery capability should consider the varying delivery capability and the varying delivery speed of items available on the shelf or obtained elsewhere. A library's capability of delivering documents to other libraries as well as to its immediate users should be considered.

2.2.7.1   Advantages.

A. These tests are not subject to user inconsistency or subjectivity.
B. They are based on objective statistical data.
C. They can generally be carried out without interrupting normal routines.
D. The measurements can be easily understood and can be compared.

E. Document Delivery Tests test not only the adequacy of collections but also the ability to deliver to the user.

2.2.7.2   Disadvantages.

A. The test procedures may not fit all libraries equally.
B. Conditions in a library may invalidate test assumptions.
C. Test samples may not be typical of overall document delivery.
D. The Document Delivery Test results are meaningful only when compared with Document Delivery Test results in other libraries or in other units or areas of the same library.

2.3   Conclusion.

In any evaluation of a library collection, a combination of these procedures may be used, the one complementing or verifying the other. Some tend to be quantitative, some qualitative, both together possibly producing a reasonable, reliable result. Finally, accurate, detailed records of the evaluation should be kept for future reference; this will avoid unnecessary duplication of effort.

Guidelines for the Review of Library Collections

1. INTRODUCTION

1.1   Purpose.

These *Guidelines* are intended to assist librarians in achieving the goal of selecting material for relegation (see definitions below), preservation, or discard in ways that are consistent with the mission of a particular library. The goals of such a review program may be centered in immediate or long-term local needs or necessities, or may be involved with the sharing of resources by libraries, or a combination of these.

Use of these *Guidelines* should be informed by the Mission and Goals and Collection Development Policy Statements of the library or collection, and by information from collection evaluations or analyses (see the preceding *Guidelines for the Formulation of Collection Development Policies* and *Guidelines for the Evaluation of the Effectiveness of Library Collections*).

1.2   Objectives.

The *Guidelines* are to serve as a tool which will guide librarians in the review of collections for relegation, preservation, or discard, and which will help them clarify objectives to staff, users, and cooperating institutions. A working bibliography has been appended, roughly divided by subject, to extend and elaborate on topics briefly covered below.

1.3   Need.

Most libraries are or will soon be faced by problems of change of institutional goals or programs, space limitation, increasing collection size and cost, the impact of new programs or needs, the problem of accumulation of duplicates or obsolescent materials which may no longer be needed in the active collection, and by the aging and decay of library materials. There is no single, or simple, answer to any of these problems, but most of them can be alleviated or reduced by a systematic, judicious, ongoing program of collection review to identify items which may require conservation treatment, or which — for a variety of reasons — may no longer be required in the active collection. Materials review will provide better collection control, provide easier access to collections, and may achieve economies of space and reduce pressures requiring additional campus facilities.

For purposes of accreditation, evidence of materials review procedures and evidence of the results of review activity may indicate sound library practice despite possible reduction in size of collection.

1.4   Scope.

These *Guidelines* are designed to aid libraries of all kinds and sizes in considering and in formulating review policies, though certain elements of the *Guidelines* will be more applicable to larger libraries.

1.5   Audience.

Library staff and administrators involved in collection development, maintenance, and preservation.

1.6   Methodology.

These *Guidelines* have been developed from review and study of the literature (see bibliography), from input and comment from committee members and consultants, from professional colleagues, and from comment at workshop sessions of the 1977 ALA Collection Development Preconference.

1.7   Definitions.

Active collection: That portion of a library's total collections immediately available in regular, staffed, campus library facilities.

Compact storage: Storage that will accommodate more books or other library materials in a given area than will a conventional stack arrangement. A density of greater than twenty volumes per square foot is considered compact storage for books. Items so stored must normally be retrieved by paging.

Demand: Request by a patron for specific materials.

Discard: The official removal of an item from either the active or low-use storage collections. Items discarded should be disposed of in an appropriate manner.

Materials: All appropriate library media including books, serials, periodicals, microform, etc. to which the principle of systematic review is applied.

Need: Materials for which there is, or it is anticipated there will be, demand or use by library clientele.

Relegation: Removal of materials from the active collection and consignment thereof to low-use storage.

Review (of library collections): Systematic examination of library collections which may result in the removal of items from the active collection for low-use storage, discard, or preservation treatment.

Shelf time (time between uses): The period of time a book remains on the shelf between circulations.

Storage: An inactive collection of little-used materials housed in a library or in remote facilities. The low-use storage area may have conventional shelving or compact storage that will accommodate more materials in a given space than conventional stack arrangement.

Use: The removal of a book from the shelf by or for a patron. Use is conventionally measured through circulation, reshelving, or a variety of more sophisticated measures or models described in the literature.

1.8   Assumptions.

A. Perhaps the major question regarding a library's collection is its adequacy in meeting the present and future needs of its clientele. If this adequacy can be increased by review of collections for relegation, preservation, or discard, then it should be done. Mature collections normally require such activity more urgently than do young collections.

B. Institutional mission and goals, size of collection, and rate of collection growth will suggest the need for review for relegation or discard. If a library can identify present or eventual problems of storage or preservation of collections, it may be advantageous to develop goals and plans for a collection review program.

C. Removal of lower priority, less acutely needed, or infrequently used materials from active collection areas may improve accessibility of the collections and reduce overall costs.

D. Reasonably timely secondary access to works seldom needed or used by patrons may not prevent successful research work.

E. For some libraries or fields of study, such as public libraries and undergraduate or science collections, measurement of circulation or demand and in-house use may be the best way to evaluate a book's value to patrons. For other libraries or collections, such as research libraries or humanities collections, assessment of patron need, disciplinary importance as evidenced by citation, or other qualitative criteria may also be significant in evaluating an item's value.

F. It is desirable to standardize terminology so as to allow comparability of practice between libraries.

G. A set of guidelines may speak to the following concerns frequently voiced when review is proposed: (a) unforeseen need for books discarded or stored may arise; (b) if a library's records show a decrease in the number of volumes held, budgets may be cut; (c) cost of a review program may be prohibitive; and (d) suitable means for the transfer or disposal of library materials may be lacking.

2. GUIDELINES

2.1 Principles.

There can be no best way to review collections for relegation, preservation, or discard. Institutional goals and programs, space limitations, and characteristics of the library clientele and collections form a web of circumstances which may be unique for each library. All these principles will be treated in order to clarify the issues involved in collection review so that realistic review goals may be formulated which are based on the combination of principles best suited to local circumstances.

2.1.1 Institutional mission, goals, and programs.

A library decision to review collections and subsequent low-use storage, discard, or treatment of materials should not be an independent activity, but should implement or follow written library policies and procedures (c.f. sections 1.1, 1.3, 1.8) which are themselves closely related to the mission, goals, and programs of the institution or clientele served by the library, available resources, and inter-institutional considerations. Collection review programs, like all library policies and procedures, should be reviewed at regular inter-vals to insure that they take into account changes in mission, goals, and programs, and are consonant with budgetary and space consider-ations. Collection review programs, for example, must remain compatible with priorities stated by the current version of the library's collection development policy. In addition, it may be desirable for a library to coordinate its review policy with those of other cooperating libraries, whether in a hierarchy or equal division of responsibilities. Such institutions may also share coordinated collection development programs or storage facilities.

2.1.1.1   Institutional goals vary greatly from one kind or size of library to another. While any library wishes its collections to be accessible to its clientele, the means of achieving this goal will vary from library to library. Each library must define accessibility and availability in terms of its goals and capacities before developing a review policy.

2.1.1.2   Support of research is a major goal of many academic libraries, with the result that in certain areas of specialization, such as the Humani-ties, an academic library may wish to retain a significant percentage of published work in the field; if space becomes limited, this goal of research may conflict with the availability of space.

2.1.1.3   Aging and deterioration of library collections is increasingly recog-nized as a problem (e.g., Library of Congress and Columbia Univer-sity have reported that approximately one-third of their collections have become seriously embrittled; the 1959 Barrow Laboratory Study of a sampling of nonfiction books printed in the U.S. between 1900 and 1939 indicated that 97 percent had an expected useful life of 50 years or less). Libraries are consequently initiating programs of conservation and preservation which require long-term systematic review of the condition of library materials so that phased plans of action can be developed over time as funds and staff levels permit. Such review may conveniently coincide with review for low-use storage or discard; indeed, storage review may be part of a conserva-tion program.

2.1.2   External constraints.

Other factors such as physical facilities, local staffing levels and distribution, need for rapid service delivery, methods used for organization of materials, and the materials budget itself will also affect the collection review policy and should be carefully considered before goals are formulated.

2.1.3   Characteristics of clientele.

The major institutional factor determining library policy should be adequate service to library clientele, the latter likely to be determined by factors outside the control of the library. For example, the clientele of a public library may be the taxpayer of the county, city, or state. The clientele of an academic library may be the faculty, staff, and students of the local campus, all faculty and students of sister campuses within the same system; or even all faculty and students within a region or within a state. In case of conflict between service imperatives and internal library goals the areas of inconsistency must be made explicit and resolved as much as possible or the collection review effort may be paralyzed in its beginnings.

2.1.4   When a program of collection review is desirable.

If availability or accessibility of a library collection can be improved by relegation of materials from the active collection, or if present or anticipated space is or will be inadequate for storing the active collection, or if aging and decay of materials in the active collection will be accelerated by retaining materials in their present condition, then a program of review may be called for.

Many authorities regard a library collection as a living organism, and consider collection review and its results as a way of maintaining a healthy, useful, and goal-centered collection. Generally, mature collections need weeding much more than do young collections. The planned ultimate size of an active collection should be based in part on a process of review. If a library formulates its collection development goals and policy, and combines these with its growth rate, it will be in a position to project goals for a collection review program.

2.2   Criteria.

Assessment of the collection to determine which volumes should be relegated, discarded, or preserved should be based on one or more of the following criteria: use, language or publication/accession date, value/quality criteria, shelf reading/book slip method, undesirable duplication, or journal relegation criteria. The relative importance assigned each factor will be determined by local need.

2.2.1   Use criteria.

Use criteria should include circulation data, shelf time, in-house use, interlibrary loan circulations, and patron consultation. All of these should probably be included to get an accurate reflection of collection use, although some are difficult to measure. A library may wish to perform a study to determine which, if any, of these measures are useful predictors of the others. In any attempt to measure use, newly published and acquired books should be excluded from use assessment during their first two years.

2.2.1.1   Circulation counts are a significant measure to be considered in developing review procedures, but circulation represents only a portion of total usage. (*See below* shelf time, in-house use, interlibrary loan, patron consultation.) Circulations are countable in most libraries and are counted in many, the measure being the number of charge-outs over a period of time. A criterion based on this measure alone would require only the assignment of a cutoff point which would define items circulating less than an assigned number of times during a specified time period as candidates for storage or discard. For example, such a decision might involve storing all books not circulated during a five-year period.

However, the following limitations to using circulation counts should be kept in mind: (a) if a library does not keep consistent circulation records of some sort over an extended period of time, a check on past circulation is extremely difficult, (b) it may be important for some libraries to measure browsing and other nonrecorded use and determine its relationship to recorded use, (c) a library could in this way abandon its responsibility to those who need to refer to little-used materials.

2.2.1.2   Shelf time. In heavily used collections it may not be possible to develop use criteria based on circulation counts alone, for very few items may fail to circulate. In this case, shelf time may prove a useful secondary tool to define potential volumes for relegation. When the time between uses exceeds an established standard, those volumes may be considered for relegation. They would still remain available to the patron, but would cease to congest the active collection.

2.2.1.3   In-house use is that aspect of total usage most difficult to measure. If we assume that areas of high circulation will also be areas of high volume in-house use, as McGrath suggested, then criteria based on circulation counts might provide adequate review guides without in-house data. Other studies such as Urquhart and Urquhart, however, suggest that this may not be the case. In a library with large non-circulating collections, in-house use will have to be measured: in such a case reshelving counts are probably the best available approximation of use information, even though studies reveal that as few as 22 percent of titles consulted in a given area may be left on the table for reshelving. In addition, many libraries do not circulate periodicals, and some combination of data derived from reshelving counts, missing issues, mutilation rates, and photocopy records may provide the desired data.

2.2.1.4   Interlibrary loan circulations are seldom recorded either by the circulation system or on the book's date due slip, but records are inevitably maintained by interlibrary loan operation for control of the flow of material. Because libraries may vary widely in the volume of interlibrary loan activity they support (loaning local material) or initiate (requesting unavailable material from other libraries), such data should be incorporated into the use measure chosen.

2.2.1.5   Patron consultation is a way of verifying that review procedures and specific selections for relegation or discard are consonant with the needs and programs of the library. While in most cases librarians are the ultimate authorities in review activities, careful consultation may prevent costly and embarrassing mistakes.

2.2.2   Estimated use.

For libraries that have no records of past circulations, it may be possible to relegate titles to storage based on such factors as language of publication, accession date, publication date, or subject field.

2.2.3   Value/quality criteria method.

Some academic, research, or special libraries may wish to review collections on the basis of the value of individual monograph titles as determined by their appearance on standard lists and/or by the judgment of a specialist or group of specialists. Criteria for value/quality review should be the same as those used initially for book selection, reflecting the goals and objectives of the library. Criteria and methodology may resemble those recommended earlier in the *Guidelines for the Evaluation of the Effectiveness of Library Collections.* In considering a volume the selector may wish to bear in mind such factors as subject matter, historical importance, age, cost, physical condition, citation in other publications, the availability of other material in the field, and the frequency of use.

For example, responsibility for value/quality review for librarians, subject specialists, and teaching faculty in an academic institution might include any of the following: (a) decision by librarian and/or subject specialist only; (b) direct faculty examination of books and production of a call number listing of those which faculty think can be stored or discarded; (c) librarian and/or subject specialist decisions subject to faculty review, which requires display of the books for a designated period of time during which faculty may remove volumes that should remain in the primary working collections; and (d) faculty selection with review by librarians and/or subject specialist.

2.2.4   Shelf reading and book slip method.

This is a method to help research or special libraries which may need to retain material without active circulation records in the active collection.

Librarians or faculty select duplicate, low-use, or little needed titles as candidates for relegation or discard through a systematic shelf-reading program. As this is done, each reviewer places a colored, appropriately labelled, and easily seen slip in each book identified as a candidate for relegation. The slip contains the call number, a legend informing a patron of the intended action, and indicates that a patron who considers the action unwise may remove the slip and turn it in at the circulation desk upon leaving the stack/library. Slips are left in books for a significant period of time (e.g., one or two years), and at the end of the fixed period all titles with slips remaining are pulled and processed for the appropriate action.

2.2.5   Undesirable duplication.

It may be important to monitor duplicates during shelf readings. Multiple copies of obsolete textbooks or other superseded books may occupy a significant proportion of badly needed shelf space in stack areas and may be controlled by a program of shelf or shelf list review.

2.2.6   Journal relegation criteria.

2.2.6.1   For journals that circulate, past use and publication date are the major criteria recommended to determine a cutoff point. Use patterns can often determine the "family quality" of journals (the use patterns of all volumes of a journal are often similar, and use is therefore usually distributed throughout a set, rather than being centered on one or two volumes).

2.2.6.2   For noncirculating journal titles, librarians often base decisions on published studies which have shown that citations of articles may be taken as a measure of use of the journals. Many of these studies show that the number of citations can be linked with the age of the journal in formulae for predicting when a journal can be relegated to storage. To be useful, obsolescence rates must be based on data collected from one's own library, because each library has a unique group of users, a unique purpose, and a unique set of physical facilities (see also 2.2.1.3).

2.2.7   Deteriorating materials criteria.

Any library must ensure that materials acquired for use by its clientele are physically sound. Each library needs a program for the identification and removal over time, as resources permit, of unsound, aged, dilapidated, or embrittled volumes from the shelves for conservation/preservation treatment. As these volumes are identified during collection review processes, a conservation/preservation program can be developed which takes into account the number of items requiring care by type and acuity of need, and time frames and cost projections can be projected for conservation treatment, photocopy, or microform replacement. In some cases, such volumes may be candidates for discard if use and other criteria indicate that they are unused or little used and available through interlibrary borrowing arrangements.

2.3   Conclusion.

Depending on the existence of available facilities for a low-use collection, a library may elect to relegate items to storage, to discard them, or, more commonly, choose some combination of storage and discard considered optimal for local conditions. In developing a review program for relegation and discard, it is important to determine the time frame for review process, and how often the cycle should be repeated. If funds and/or staffing permit, collection review should be made an ongoing program, integrating relegation and discard with the purchase of new materials. In most cases, however, it will be possible to review only at times when the pressures of regular work subside or projected space problems make such a program necessary.

Once a review program has been established, review criteria should be chosen in accordance with the principles, cautions, and criteria discussed above. Whatever the decision, the actual methodology will be influenced by the resources available to implement any review project and the time frame adopted for its accomplishment. Criteria for the use of items in the storage collection should be assigned so as to allow the automatic and rapid return of stored items to the active collection if they receive a minimum level of use.

Guidelines for the Allocation of Library Materials Budgets

1. INTRODUCTION

1.1   Purpose.

These guidelines are offered to assist librarians in allocating funds for library materials, whether through use of a published formula or a method devised locally.

1.2   Objectives.

The Committee has attempted to bring together the elements to be considered in the allocation process. Some published formulas and allocation models which may assist in the process are described, together with a discussion of the advantages and disadvantages of using a formula.

1.3   Need.

Greater accountability for specific budget expenditures and reductions in budget size have created a climate in which the allocation of funds for library materials should be done in a manner that is both understandable and justifiable. An allocation method based on recognized criteria is more likely to meet with acceptance and approval, and it can serve as a valuable planning tool.

1.4   Scope.

The guidelines are designed to aid libraries of all kinds and sizes in determining the most useful way of allocating funds for library materials.

1.5   Audience.

These *Guidelines* are intended to assist library budget officers, collection development librarians, administrators and staff involved in the allocation of the library's materials funds. The guidelines are also intended to aid in communicating the allocation process to library users, to other library staff, and to nonlibrary administrators who have a role in budget allocation and approval.

1.6   Methodology.

These *Guidelines* were drafted by a Subcommittee of the Collection Development Committee and submitted to the full Committee in open meetings at several ALA Midwinter and Annual Conferences. During this same period, the Committee sponsored a program on the allocation of book funds at the Annual Conference in 1974; and at one of its meetings at the Annual Conference in July 1975, it invited several visitors with experience in the development of allocation formulas to share their methods and ideas with members of the Committee. Further revision followed the 1977 Collection Development Preconference in Detroit. These, and subsequent group discussions, led to extensive revisions of the initial draft of the guidelines.

1.7   Definitions.

1.7.1   *Allocation*: Assignment of a portion of the library materials budget to a particular subject field, type of material, administrative unit, etc.

1.7.2   *Allocation unit*: Unit to which an allocation is made; e.g., department, subject LC category. In statistical terms, it is one of the quantities in a variable and is called the *unit of analysis*.

1.7.3   *Approval plans*: Materials are supplied by a vendor or publisher, based upon an individual profile of library needs. Items may be selected or rejected by appropriate library staff.

1.7.4   *Budget*: Funds assigned to the library, usually with a certain portion earmarked for the purchase of library materials.

1.7.5   *Evaluation*: Assessment, preferably periodic, of the effectiveness of a particular allocation method in achieving a library's collection goals.

1.7.6   *Factor*: A concept that may or may not be quantifiable. Generally, much vaguer and more difficult to define than variable (see below). A factor may include several variables.

1.7.7   *Formula*: A mathematical model based on prescribed variables for assisting in distribution of library funds.

1.7.8   *Library materials*: All items which make up the holdings of a library. These can include books, manuscripts, serials, government publications, recordings, microforms, pamphlets, maps, etc.

1.7.9   *Monitoring*: Regular checking on the status and use of the allocations provided from the library materials budget.

1.7.10 *Standing order*: An order to a vendor or publisher to supply automatically, as published, all publications in a particular series or in a work-in-parts.

1.7.11 *Test of effectiveness*: Any means used to examine the results of the allocation process and by which an evaluation is made.

1.7.12 *Variable*: A unit which varies quantitatively, such as the number of students enrolled in a department, or the number of books in a subject.

1.7.13 *Weighting*: Assigning a level of value or importance to a specified variable such as the number of full-time equivalency undergraduates. Weights may be assigned arbitrarily to reflect administrative policy. Or they may be determined empirically by computing a variable's relationship to a criterion variable, such as the relationship of enrollment to circulation.

1.8   Assumptions.

1.8.1   A rational method for the allocation of funds for library materials is desirable and achievable. Each institution will need to develop its own method for allocation which will apply to its own circumstance; however, existing formulas can be (and have been) used as models to assist individual institutions in this process. If properly designed, the allocation method should:

1.8.1.1 Open up the allocation process and identify assumptions.

1.8.1.2 Provide for a planned and logical distribution of available funds, based on the library's goals and priorities.

1.8.1.3 Enable the library to monitor expenditures of funds.

1.8.1.4 Enable the library to demonstrate to both fiscal authorities and patrons how money is being allocated and spent.

1.8.1.5   Provide a method for fulfilling collection goals and needs, as well as institutional goals.

1.8.1.6   Allow increments which will allow desired levels of programmatic support.

1.8.2   In a climate of budget restraints and tighter fiscal control, it becomes increasingly desirable to use some method of allocation, even if one was not used in the past, to insure that all parts of the collection receive consideration and an appropriate share of the funds.

1.8.3   In an era of resource-sharing, a rational method for the allocation of funds can help to insure that the needs of one's institution are being met without the unnecessary overlap or duplication with other institutions.

2. GUIDELINES

2.1   Principles.

2.1.1   Any method used should provide for an effective distribution of available funds, according to agreed-upon priorities.

2.1.2   Librarians, with appropriate consultation, should allocate funds.

2.1.3   The allocation method should be developed in conjunction with the library's goals and collection development policy.

2.1.4   The allocation method should be readily understandable to those who are responsible for the administration and expenditure of such funds.

2.1.5   The allocation method should be flexible enough to respond to changing circumstances or needs within the institution, changes in the publishing industry or book market, and unexpected opportunities for special purchases.

2.1.6   The allocation process should allow for both present needs and anticipated future needs, thus assisting in the planning process.

2.1.7   The allocation method used should be sufficiently well designed and objective not to be readily subject to political pressure.

2.1.8   The allocation process should be one which can provide better program support.

2.2   Factors to be considered in selecting an allocation method.

2.2.1   Whether there is now a formal budgeting process which may place constraints on, or limit the choices of, an allocation method.

2.2.2   Whether the type of accounting procedure or other institutional regulations in use may limit the options; e.g., whether there are encumbrances, whether unspent funds can be carried forward or transferred from one account to another.

2.2.3   Whether an institution is in a "steady state," in a period of growth, or in a period of reduction.

2.2.4   Whether the necessary data are available, e.g., circulation figures.

2.2.5   Whether there exists a formal or informal policy statement and/or statement of priorities.

2.3   Methods of allocating library materials funds.

It is probable that no one method is, or can be, used exclusively within a single institution and that a combination may be necessary. Many budgets provide specific sums of money for certain categories of material (e.g., monographs, serials, newspapers, microforms) for individual units of the library (e.g., a branch library, reference department), or for specific subject fields or language areas.

2.3.1   Allocation units and their advantages and disadvantages.

2.3.1.1   By broad subject field, e.g., humanities, social sciences.
Advantages: Allows flexibility.
Disadvantages: A small subject within the broader one may be overlooked or treated inequitably.

2.3.1.2   By specific subject field, e.g., anthropology.
Advantages: It is easy to monitor behavior in a particular category.
Disadvantages: Interdisciplinary materials cannot be assigned so specifically; specific items may not be identifiable in standing orders or approval plans.

2.3.1.2.1 By major LC or Dewey schedule, e.g., A, B, BC, 010, 020, etc.
Advantages: Acquisition rate could be correlated with largest libraries, such as LC, and thus with national or worldwide publishing rates in each category.
Disadvantages: Could not be correlated readily with institutional policy, curriculum, or academic emphasis.

2.3.1.2.2   By subject profile of academic departments, based on LC or Dewey analysis of courses.
Advantages: Possible to relate acquisitions directly to programs or curriculum.
Disadvantages: Can be difficult to construct profile and collect necessary data.

2.3.1.3   By form of material, e.g., monographs, serials, microform.
Advantages: Statistical data for library and government agencies are usually based on this type of information.
Disadvantages: The subject breakdown possibility may be lost. Flexibility also may be lost.

2.3.1.4   To units within the library, e.g., reference department, branch.
Advantages: Enables unit to develop an appropriate collection based on user needs since there is a close relationship between the department and its users. Greater accountability is possible.
Disadvantages: Duplication of interdisciplinary materials will be required. While duplication is not necessarily undesirable, it will be necessary to have a mechanism to insure that unnecessary duplication is avoided.

2.3.1.5   To academic department or program, e.g., Philosophy, English.
Advantages: Faculty members are involved in the selection process.
Disadvantages: The library risks spotty, unsystematic, and inconsistent development of collections over time.

2.4   Allocation, monitoring, control.
All the individuals and groups mentioned below may be involved to some extent in all parts of the allocation process, but the most usual assignments of responsibility are as follows:

2.4.1   Allocation is done by:
Chief Librarian or other administrative officer
Collection Development Officer
Head of Acquisitions
Staff and/or administrative committee
Cooperative effort between library and faculty committee or departments.

2.4.2   Monitoring of expenditures is done by:
Collection Development Officer

Bibliographer
Acquisitions Librarian
Faculty or academic department.

2.4.3   Evaluation of the allocation method is done by:
Collection Development Officer
Staff committee
Selection personnel
Users: students, staff, other users. This could involve direct or indirect input.

2.5   Problem areas in determining allocations.

2.5.1   Coverage of standing orders, approval, or blanket order plans may be interdisciplinary, thus a subject breakdown is difficult. Also, the required budget amount for these may be difficult to determine in advance.

2.5.2   If there are separate budgets for serials, newspapers, microforms, etc., it may force rigidity on what should be a flexible process.

2.5.3   There is almost always a need for a discretionary fund to take advantage of opportunities or to give aid in a crisis.

2.5.4   The impact of new programs requiring start-up funds can put the budget out of balance, if such funds were not sought or provided in advance.

2.5.5   Duplication in certain categories of materials may be necessary or desirable. Special allowances have to be made for this.

2.5.6   Retrospective material may be needed, but the availability of such materials and their actual costs may be hard to predict.

2.5.7   Inflation factors must be taken into consideration.

2.5.8   The quantity and cost of publications in various subjects or languages may vary widely and should be taken into account in determining allocations.

2.5.9   Gifts and exchange materials can have an impact on allocation funds and may fill the need for certain materials so that purchase is not needed. Budget flexibility to transfer funds from an area where they are not needed will help deal with this situation.

2.5.10   Special funds may have special requirements or limitations on their use. They may even be sufficient to wholly support certain areas of the collection. These must be taken into consideration when regular funds are allocated.

2.5.11   A windfall of funds late in the fiscal year can disrupt the carefully planned allocation process. A procedure for insuring that such funds are wisely spent is essential, e.g., keeping a file of lower priority but approved items to be purchased if additional funds become available.

2.6   Considerations in the development of allocation methods.

2.6.1   Objective factors.

2.6.1.1   External (publishing and book trade) considerations.
           A. The rate and pattern of publishing in various subjects or geographical areas, or for various types of materials
           B. Costs of books and other materials
           C. Differences in costs between various categories of materials
           D. Inflation.

2.6.1.2   Internal (library) considerations.
           A. Size of the collection
           B. Rate of growth of the collection (by subject, department, etc.)
           C. Use of the collection
           D. Unfilled patron needs
           E. Interlibrary borrowing and lending statistics.

2.6.1.3   Nature and size of user group.
           A. Campus:
               Institutional mission
               Method of instruction
               Faculty size, composition, and quality
               Citation level of faculty
               Student enrollment
               Credit hours
               Graduate programs
               Degrees granted
               Off-campus users
               Research programs
               Publications
               Remoteness from or proximity to other libraries
               Cooperative agreements.

B. Public library:
Library use intensity
Number of users
Composition of users
Literacy level.
C. Special library:
Employees
Outside users
Research staff
Contractors.
D. School library:
Students
Faculty
Staff.

2.6.2   Subjective considerations.

A. Goals of the institution
B. Politics (campus, city, county, state, business, etc.)
C. Historical development of the collection
D. Academic distinction of departments in college or university
E. Extent of reliance of academic department or discipline on library materials.

2.6.3   Weighting of above factors.

There is no generally recognized standard for weighting the above factors. The weight given to a particular factor in a library will be determined by the goals and resources of the library, and will be tailored to the individual library. Many institutions determine their own weightings; e.g., enrollment in upper division units is worth two of lower division units. Others simply weigh all factors in formula equally.

2.7   Published formulas and allocation methods which may be used in the allocation process.

Formulas have been devised to allocate funds among institutions (e.g., the Washington Formula), and within a single institution (e.g., McGrath Formula). Some, such as the Kohut model, address a specific problem—in this case, the balancing of serial and monographic purchases. Brief descriptions and citations to the full texts of the following formulas are provided in Appendix B: Dillehay, Gold, Kohut, McGrath, Pierce.

2.8   Using a formula.

A library may decide to develop its own allocation model or to use one of the models described. It is important to understand what a formula can and cannot do.

2.8.1   Why use a formula?

An appropriate formula may provide for a logical and more equitable distribution of available funds. It can also assist in creating a budget based on programs, priorities, and goals of the institution. It can assist in making choices, so that choosing alternatives and priorities becomes an articulated rather than an unclear process. A good formula can be quite flexible, if properly designed. However, adoption of a formula should not imply rigid acceptance of it.

2.8.2   What can a formula be used for?

It can be used for an initial allocation of funds, for a reallocation of funds, or to allocate supplementary funds to the base.

2.8.3   Benefits of using a formula.

Once a suitable formula has been developed, funds can be allocated easily and quickly. Allocations can be justified on the basis of the formula and objectivity in the allocation process can be demonstrated. The formula itself can be reexamined periodically, if necessary. A formula is equitable, limits variables and factors, and provides structure.

2.8.4   Disadvantages of using a formula.

A formula may not be flexible enough to cover differing needs in various areas, e.g., absolute equity may not be desirable. A formula may not allow for sudden changes in fiscal circumstances. The data necessary for the development of a formula may not be readily available, e.g., library's own book cost figures or data on the rate of publishing in the various subject fields. A formula could be used by budgetary authorities to deny as well as to provide funds. In fact, using a formula may be more difficult and more time-consuming for at least two reasons: (1) if data are plugged in freshly each year, the data must be collected and analyzed in order to determine appropriate weights; and (2) if a departmental subject profile is used, the profile must be revised each year. If the formula is not reviewed each year and the same weights are used, the formula could become stale. A formula may limit variables and thus produce an inappropriate result.

2.8.5   Problems not yet handled by any library budget formula.

      A.   Retrospective acquisition rates.

      B.   Built-in recovery from lean years.

      C.   Recognition of existing collection adequacy.

      D.   Rates of literature obsolescence in all disciplines. However, half-lives of journal literature, a measure of obsolescence, have been computed for several disciplines.

      E.   Intuition and knowledge based on experience, e.g., subjective judgment.

      F.   Multiple copies.

      G.   Replacement materials.

      H.   Quality of expenditures.

2.9   Assessment of the efficacy of the allocation process.

Testing the effectiveness of any allocation method should be a regular or periodic operation. Each year's budget preparation should include a review and evaluation of the results of the preceding year's allocations. Methods for evaluation include the use of circulation statistics, interlibrary loan statistics, comparison with bibliographies, user comment and opinion, unfilled patron needs, and the rate and pattern of collection growth.

Titles Classified by the Library of Congress Classification: National Shelflist Count

AC		Collections
AE		Encyclopedias
AG		General Reference Works
AI		Indexes
AM		Museums, Collectors & Collecting
AN		Newspapers (if used by campus)
AP		Periodicals
AS		Societies. Academies
AY		Yearbooks. Almanacs. Directories
AZ		History of the Sciences in General. Scholarship. Learning
B	1-68	Philosophy: Periodicals, Societies, Congresses, etc.
B	69-789	Philosophy: History and Systems, Ancient through Renaissance
B	790-5739	Philosophy: History and Systems, Post-Renaissance
BC		Logic
BD		Speculative Philosophy
BF	1-1000	Psychology
BF	1001-1400	Parapsychology
BF	1401-1999	Occult Sciences
BH		Aesthetics
BJ	1-1800	Ethics
BJ	1801-2195	Social Usages, Etiquette
BL		Religions. Mythology. Rationalism
BM		Judaism

BP		Islam. Bahaism. Theosophy, etc.
BQ		Buddhism
BR		Christianity (General)
BS		Bible
BT		Doctrinal Theology
BV		Practical Theology
BX	1-799	Eastern Christian Churches
BX	800-4795	Roman Catholic Church
BX	4800-9999	Protestantism
C		Auxiliary Sciences of History: General
CB		History of Civilization and Culture
CC		Archaeology (General)
CD		Diplomatics. Archives. Seals
CE		Chronology
CJ		Numismatics
CN		Epigraphy
CR		Heraldry
CS		Genealogy
CT		Biography
D	1-900	History (General)
D	901-1075	History of Europe, General
DA		History: Great Britain
DB		History: Austria, Austro-Hungarian Empire, Hungary
DC		History: France
DD		History: Germany
DE		History: Mediterranean Region, Greco-Roman World
DF		History: Greece
DG		History: Italy
DH		History: Netherlands (Low Countries, General and Belgium)
DJ		History: Netherlands (Holland)
DJK		History: Eastern Europe
DK		History: Russia, U.S.S.R.
DL		History: Northern Europe, Scandinavia
DP	1-500	History: Spain
DP	501-900	History: Portugal
DQ		History: Switzerland
DR		History: Eastern Europe. Balkan Peninsula
DS	1-40	History: Asia
DS	41-329	History: Southwestern Asia, Ancient Orient, Near East

DS	330-500	History: Southern Asia, Indian Ocean
DS	501-935	History: Eastern Asia, Southeastern Asia, Far East
DT		History: Africa
DU		History: Oceania (South Seas)
DX		History: Gypsies

E	1-139	History of Americas: General, Indians, North America
E	140-200	United States, Colonial, Special Topics
E	201-299	United States, Revoluntionary Period
E	301-440	United States, 1790-1855
E	441-655	United States, Slavery and Civil War
E	656-867	United States Since the Civil War

F	1-205	State & Local History: New England, Atlantic Coast
F	206-475	State & Local History: South, Gulf States
F	476-705	State & Local History: Midwest, Mississippi Valley
F	721-854	State & Local History: The West
F	856-975	State & Local History: Pacific Coast, Alaska
F	1000-1170	History: British America, Canada
F	1201-1392	History: Mexico
F	1401-1419	History: Latin America, Spanish America (General)
F	1421-1577	History: Central America
F	1601-2151	History: West Indies
F	2155-2183	History: Caribbean Area
F	2201-3799	History: South America

G	1-922	Geography (General)
G	1001-3122	Atlases
G	3160-9980	Maps
GA	1-87	Mathematical Geography
GA	100-1999	Cartography
GB		Physical Geography
GC		Oceanography
GF		Anthropogeography
GN	1-296	Anthropology
GN	301-686	Ethnology and Ethnography
GN	700-875	Prehistoric Archaeology
GR		Folklore
GT		Manners and Customs (General)
GV	1-200	Recreation
GV	201-555	Physical Training

GV	557-1198	Sports
GV	1199-1570	Games and Amusements
GV	1580-1799	Dancing
GV	1800-1860	Circuses, Carnivals, etc.
H		The Social Sciences in General
HA		Statistics
HB		Economic Theory
HC		Economic History & Conditions: National Production
HD	1-100	Economics: Production
HD	101-1395	Economics: Land
HD	1401-2210	Agricultural Economics
HD	2321-4730	Economics: Industry
HD	4801-8942	Labor
HD	9000-9999	Special Industries and Trades
HE		Transportation and Communication
HF	1-4050	Commerce
HF	5001-6351	Business
HG		Finance
HJ		Public Finance
HM		Sociology: General Works, Theory
HN		Sociology: Social History and Conditions, etc.
HQ		Family, Marriage, Woman, Sexual Life
HS		Societies: Secret, Benevolent, etc.
HT		Communities, Classes, Races
HV		Social Pathology, Welfare, Criminology
HX		Socialism, Communism, Anarchism, Utopianism
J		Official Documents
JA		Political Science: Collections, etc.
JC		Political Theory
JF		Constitutional History, Administration: General, Comparative
JK		Constitutional History & Administration: United States
JL		Constitutional History, Admin.: British and Latin America
JN		Constitutional History & Administration: Europe
JQ		Constitutional Hist., Admin.: Asia, Africa, Australia, Oceania
JS		Local Government
JV	1-5399	Colonies and Colonization
JV	6001-9500	Emigration & Immigration
JX		International Law

K-KC	Law: General
KD	Law: United Kingdom and Ireland
KE	Law: Canada
KF	Law: U.S. (Federal)
KFA-KFW	Law: U.S. States and Territories
KFX	Law: U.S. Cities
KFZ	Law of Individual Territories
KG-KX	Law: Latin America and Old World

L	Education—General
LA	History of Education
LB	Theory & Practice of Education
LC	Special Aspects of Education
LD	Education: Individual Institutions: United States
LE	Education: Institutions: America (Except United States)
LF	Education: Individual Institutions: Europe
LG	Education: Institutions: Asia, Africa, Oceania
LH	College & School Magazines and Papers
LJ	Student Fraternities and Societies
LT	Textbooks

M	1-4	Music: Collections, Manuscripts, Collected Works, etc.
M	5-1490	Instrumental Music, Music Before 1700
M	1495-5000	Vocal Music
ML		Literature of Music
MT		Musical Instruction and Study

N	Visual Arts (General)
NA	Architecture
NB	Sculpture
NC	Graphic Arts (General), Drawing, Design
ND	Painting
NE	Print Media: Printmaking, Engraving, Lithography, etc.
NK	Decorative Arts, Applied Arts, Crafts
NX	Arts in General

P		Philology, Linguistics
PA	1-2995	Classical Philology
PA	3000-3049	Classical Literature
PA	3050-4500	Greek Literature
PA	5000-5665	Byzantine & Modern Greek Literature
PA	6000-7041	Latin Literature

PA	8001-8595	Medieval and Modern Latin Literature
PB	1-431	Modern Languages: General
PB	1001-3029	Celtic Languages and Literatures
PC	1-400	Romanic Philology and Languages: General
PC	601-872	Romanian Language and Literature
PC	890	Dalmatian
PC	901-986	Raeto-Romance Language and Literature
PC	1001-1984	Italian Language, Sardinian Language & Literature
PC	2001-3761	French Language
PC	3801-3976	Catalan Language and Literature
PC	4001-4977	Spanish Language
PC	5001-5498	Portuguese Language
PD	1-777	Germanic Philology and Languages: General
PD	1001-1350	Old Germanic Dialects
PD	1501-7159	North Germanic, Scandinavian
PE		English Philology and Language
PF	1-979	Dutch Language
PF	1001-1184	Flemish Language
PF	1401-1558	Friesian Language and Literature
PF	3001-5999	German Language
PG	1-489	Slavic Philology: General
PG	500-585	Slavic Literature: General
PG	601-799	Church Slavic
PG	801-1158	Bulgarian Language and Literature
PG	1161-1164	Macedonian Language and Literature
PG	1171-1798	Serbo-Croatian Language and Literature
PG	1801-1998	Slovenian Language and Literature
PG	2001-2850	Russian Language
PG	2900-3155	Russian Literature: History and Criticism
PG	3200-3299	Russian Literature: Collections
PG	3300-3490	Russian Literature: Individual Authors
PG	3500-3560	Russian Literature: Provincial and Local
PG	3561-3800	Subjects other than Russian Literature
PG	3801-3998	Ukrainian Language and Literature
PG	4001-5198	Czech Language and Literature
PG	5201-5598	Slovak Language and Literature
PG	5631-5698	Sorbian Language and Literature
PG	6001-7498	Polish Language and Literature
PG	7900-7948	Minor Slavic Dialects
PG	8001-9263	Baltic Languages

PG 9501-9678	Albanian
PH 1-79	Finno-Ugrian and Basque: General
PH 91-498	Finnish Language and Literature
PH 501-1109	Other Finnish Languages and Dialects
PH 1201-3718	Hungarian, Ugrian Languages and Literature
PH 5001-5490	Basque Language and Literature
PJ 1-995	Oriental Philology and Literature: General
PJ 1001-1989	Egyptology
PJ 2001-2199	Coptic
PJ 2301-2551	Hamitic
PJ 3001-4091	Semitic Philology, Assyrian, Sumerian
PJ 4101-5809	Hebrew, Aramaic, Syriac
PJ 5901-9288	Arabic, Ethiopian
PK 1-90	Indo-Iranian Philology and Literature: General
PK 101-2891	Indo-Aryan Languages
PK 2901-5534	Indo-Aryan Literature
PK 6001-6599	Iranian Philology and Literature
PK 6701-6996	Afghan, Beluchi, Kurdish, Ossetic, etc.
PK 7001-9601	Dardic, Armenian, Caucasian Languages
PL 1-489	Ural-Altaic Languages
PL 490-495	East Asiatic Languages & Literature (General), Ainu
PL 501-898	Japanese Language and Literature
PL 901-998	Korean Language and Literature
PL 1001-3299	Chinese Language and Literature
PL 3301-3505	Non-Chinese Languages of China
PL 3521-4587	Indo-Chinese, Karen, Tai, etc. Languages
PL 4601-4961	Dravidian Languages and Literature
PL 5001-7101	Oceanic Languages
PL 7501-7893	Unclassed Languages of Asia and the Pacific
PL 8000-8844	African Languages
PM 1-95	Hyperborean Languages of America and Asia
PM 101-7356	American Languages
PM 7801-7895	Mixed Languages, Creole, Pidgeon English, etc.
PM 8001-9021	Artificial Languages, Secret Languages, Esperanto, etc.
PN 1-44	Literature: Periodicals, Yearbooks, Societies, etc.
PN 45-75	Literature: Theory, Philosophy, Esthetics
PN 80-99	Literary Criticism
PN 101-249	Authorship
PN 441-1009	Literary History
PN 1010-1590	Poetry, the Performing Arts, Show Biz

PN	1600-1657	The Drama: Periodicals, Yearbooks, General Works
PN	1660-1864	Technique of Dramatic Composition, History of Drama
PN	1865-1989	Historical & Religious Plays, Tragedy, etc.
PN	1990-1992	Broadcasting
PN	1993-1999	Motion Pictures
PN	2000-2081	The Theater: General
PN	2085-2219	The Theater: The Stage, Accessories, History by Period
PN	2220-2298	The Theater in the United States
PN	2300-2554	The Theater in the Americas Except U.S.
PN	2570-2859	The Theater in Europe
PN	2860-3030	The Theater in Asia, Africa, and Oceania
PN	3035	Jewish Theater
PN	3151-3191	The Theater: Amateur and College Theatricals
PN	3195-3300	The Theater: Minstrel Shows, Spectacles, Tableaux, etc.
PN	3311-3503	Prose, Prose Fiction, the Short Story, etc.
PN	4001-4355	Oratory, Elocution, etc.
PN	4390-4500	Diaries, Letters and Essays
PN	4699-5650	Journalism and the Periodical Press
PN	6010-6078	Literature: General Collections
PN	6080-6095	Collections of Quotations
PN	6099-6120	Collections of Poetry and Drama
PN	6121-6146	Collections of Orations, Letters, Essays
PN	6147-6231	Wit and Humor, Satire
PN	6233-6381	Anacreontic Literature, Extracts, etc.
PN	6400-6700	Proverbs, etc.
PQ	1-841	French Literature: History and Criticism
PQ	1100-1297	Collections of French Literature
PQ	1300-1595	Old French Literature, to ca. 1525
PQ	1600-1709	French Literature, 16th Century
PQ	1710-1935	French Literature, 17th Century
PQ	1947-2147	French Literature, 18th Century
PQ	2149-2551	French Literature, 19th Century
PQ	2600-2651	French Literature, 1900-1960
PQ	2660-2686	French Literature, 1961-
PQ	3800-3999	French Literature, Provincial, Local, Colonial, etc.
PQ	4001-4263	Italian Literature: History and Criticism
PQ	4265-4556	Italian Literature to 1400
PQ	4561-4664	Italian Literature, 1400-1700
PQ	4675-4734	Italian Literature, 1701-1900
PQ	4800-4886	Italian Literature, 1901-

PQ	5901-5999	Italian Literature: Provincial, Local, Colonial
PQ	6001-6269	Spanish Literature: History, Criticism, Collections, etc.
PQ	6271-6498	Spanish Literature to 1700
PQ	6500-6576	Spanish Literature, 1700-ca. 1868
PQ	6600-6647	Spanish Literature, 1868-1960
PQ	6651-6676	Spanish Literature, 1961-
PQ	7000-7079	Spanish Literature: Provincial, & in Europe, North America
PQ	7080-7087	Spanish Literature in Spanish America (General)
PQ	7100-7349	Spanish Literature of Mexico, Former U.S. Spanish Provinces
PQ	7361-7539	Spanish Literature of West Indies and Central America
PQ	7551-8560	Spanish Literature of South America
PQ	8600-8929	Spanish Literature of Africa, Asia, Australia, etc.
PQ	9000-9189	Portuguese Literature: History, Criticism, Collections, etc.
PQ	9191-9255	Portuguese Literature to 1700
PQ	9261-9288	Portuguese Literature since 1700
PQ	9400-9479	Portuguese Literature: Provincial & in Europe, U.S., Canada
PQ	9500-9696	Portuguese Literature of Brazil, to 1800
PQ	9697-9699	Portuguese Literature of Brazil, since 1800
PQ	9900-9999	Portuguese Literature of Africa, Asia, Australia, etc.
PR	1-78	English Literature: Literary History and Criticism
PR	81-151	History of English Literature, General
PR	161-479	History of English Literature, by Period
PR	500-978	History of English Literature, by Form (Poetry, Drama, etc)
PR	1098-1395	English Literature: Collections
PR	1490-1799	Anglo-Saxon Literature
PR	1803-2165	Anglo-Norman and Early Middle English Literature
PR	2199-2405	English Renaissance Literature, Prose and Poetry
PR	2411-2416	English Renaissance Drama: Anonymous Plays
PR	2417-2749	English Renaissance Drama: Plays by Playwrights A-Shaj
PR	2750-3112	Shakespeare
PR	3135-3198	English Renaissance Drama: Plays by Playwrights Shar-Z
PR	3291-3785	English Literature, 17th and 18th Centuries
PR	3991-5990	English Literature, 19th Century
PR	6000-6049	English Literature, 1900-1960
PR	6050-6076	English Literature, 1961-
PR	8309-9899	English Literature: Provincial, Colonial, etc.
PS	1-478	American Literature: General, Criticism, History
PS	501-690	American Literature: Collections
PS	700-893	American Literature: Colonial Period
PS	991-3390	American Literature: 19th Century

PS	3500-3549	American Literature: 1900-1960
PS	3550-3576	American Literature: 1961-
PT	1-951	German Literature: History, Criticism, Folk Literature
PT	1100-1485	Collections of German Literature
PT	1501-1695	German Literature: 1050-1450/1500
PT	1701-1797	German Literature: 1500-ca. 1700
PT	1799-2592	German Literature: 1700-ca. 1860/70
PT	2600-2659	German Literature: 1860/70-1960
PT	2660-2688	German Literature: 1961-
PT	3701-4899	German Literature: Provincial, Local, Colonial, etc.
PT	5001-5395	Dutch Literature: History and Criticism
PT	5400-5547	Dutch Literature: Collections
PT	5555-5880	Dutch Literature through 1960
PT	5881	Dutch Literature, 1961-
PT	5885-5980	Translations into Dutch, Provincial Dutch Literature, etc.
PT	6000-6471	Flemish Literature since 1830
PT	6500-6590	Afrikaans Literature to 1960
PT	6592	Afrikaans Literature since 1961
PT	7001-7099	Scandinavian Literature: General
PT	7101-7599	Icelandic, Old Norwegian, Faroese
PT	7601-8260	Danish Literature
PT	8301-9155	Norwegian Literature
PT	9201-9999	Swedish Literature
PZ	1-4	Fiction in English
PZ	5-10	Juvenile Literature: American and English
PZ	11-99	Juvenile Literature: Foreign
Q		Science (General) (B)
QA	1-99	Mathematics (General)
QA	101-145	Arithmetic
QA	150-299	Algebra
QA	300-433	Mathematical Analysis (Calculus, etc.)
QA	440-799	Geometry, Trigonometry
QA	801-939	Analytic Mechanics
QB		Astronomy
QC	1-75	Physics (General)
QC	81-119	Weights and Measures
QC	120-168	Experimental Mechanics
QC	170-220	Constitution and Properties of Matter
QC	221-246	Sound

QC 251-338	Heat
QC 350-496	Light, Optics, Radiation (General)
QC 501-798	Electricity, Magnetism, Nuclear Physics
QC 801-999	Geophysics, Meteorology, Geomagnetism
QD 1-69	Chemistry (General)
QD 71-145	Analytical Chemistry
QD 146-199	Inorganic Chemistry
QD 241-449	Organic Chemistry
QD 450-731	Physical and Theoretical Chemistry
QD 901-999	Crystallography
QE	Geology
QH 1-199	Natural History (General)
QH 201-278	Microscopy
QH 301-705	Biology (General)
QK 1-474	Botany (General)
QK 475-989	Botany (Specific Fields)
QL 1-355	Zoology (General)
QL 362-739	Invertebrate and Vertebrate Zoology
QL 750-991	Ethology, Anatomy, Embryology
QM	Human Anatomy (B)
QP 1-348	Physiology (General) (B)
QP 351-499	Nervous System and the Senses (B)
QP 501-801	Animal Biochemistry (B)
QP 901-981	Experimental Pharmacology (B)
QR	Microbiology (B)
R 1-130	Medicine: Periodicals, Societies, General Topics (B)
R 131-687	Medicine: History, Medical Expeditions (B)
R 690-899	Medicine: Special Subjects (B)
RA 3-420	Medicine and the State (B)
RA 421-790	Public Health (B)
RA 791-955	Medical Geography
RA 960-998	Medical Centers, Hospitals, etc. (B)
RA 1001-1171	Forensic Medicine, Medical Jurisprudence (B)
RA 1190-1270	Toxicology (B)
RB	Pathology (B)
RC 1-106	Internal Medicine, Medical Practice: General Works (B)
RC 110-253	Infectious and Parasitic Diseases (B)
RC 254-298	Neoplasma, Neoplastic Diseases (B)
RC 306-320	Tuberculosis (B)

RC	321-431	Neurology (B)
RC	435-576	Psychiatry, Psychopathology (B)
RC	578-632	Allergic, Metabolic, Nutritional Diseases (B)
RC	633-935	Diseases of Organs, Glands, Systems (B)
RC	936-951	Diseases of Regions of the Body (B)
RC	952-1299	Geriatrics, Arctic and Tropical Medicine, etc. (B)
RD		Surgery (B)
RE		Ophthalmology (B)
RF		Otorhinolaryngology (B)
RG		Gynecology and Obstetrics (B)
RJ		Pediatrics (B)
RK		Dentistry (B)
RL		Dermatology (B)
RM		Therapeutics, Pharmacology (B)
RS		Pharmacy and Materia Medica (B)
RT		Nursing (B)
RV		Botanic, Thomsonian, Eclectic Medicine (B)
RX		Homeopathy (B)
RZ		Other Systems of Medicine (B)
S	1-760	Agriculture (General)
S	900-972	Conservation of Natural Resources
SB		Plant Culture and Horticulture
SD		Forestry
SF		Animal Culture, Veterinary Medicine, etc.
SH		Fish Culture and Fisheries
SK		Hunting Sports
T		Technology - General
TA		Engineering - General, Civil Engineering
TC		Hydraulic Engineering
TD		Environmental Technology, Sanitary Engineering
TE		Highway Engineering
TF		Railroad Engineering and Operation
TG		Bridge Engineering
TH		Building Construction
TJ		Mechanical Engineering and Machinery
TK		Electrical Engineering, Electronics, Nuclear Engineering
TL		Motor Vehicles, Aeronautics, Astronautics
TN		Mining Engineering and Metallurgy
TP		Chemical Technology

TR		Photography
TS		Manufactures
TT		Handicrafts, Arts and Crafts
TX		Domestic Arts
U		Military Science (General)
UA		Armies: Organization, Distribution, etc.
UB		Military Administration
UC		Military Science: Maintenance and Transportation
UD		Infantry
UE		Cavalry, Armor
UF		Artillery
UG		Military Engineering
UH		Military Science: Other Services
V		Naval Science (General)
VA		Navies: Organization, Distribution, etc.
VB		Naval Administration
VC		Naval Maintenance
VD		Naval Seamen
VE		Marines
VF		Naval Ordnance
VG		Minor Services of Navies
VK		Navigation, Merchant Marine
VM		Naval Architecture, Shipbuilding, etc.
Z	4-15	History of Books and Bookmaking
Z	40-115	Writing, Paleography
Z	116-550	Printing
Z	551-661	Copyright, Intellectual Property
Z	662-1000	Libraries: Library Science
Z	1001-1121	Bibliography, General
Z	1201-1212	National Bibliography: America
Z	1215-1361	National Bibliography: United States (B)
Z	1365-1401	National Bibliography: Canada
Z	1411-1945	National Bibliography: Mexico, Central & South America
Z	2000-2959	National Bibliography: Europe
Z	3001-4980	National Bibliography: Asia, Africa, Australia, Oceania
Z	5051-5055	Subject and Personal Bibliography: Academies, Societies, etc.
Z	5056-8999	Subject and Personal Bibliography: Other

Descriptions and Citations to Selected Formulas

MC GRATH FORMULA

McGrath, William E. "A Pragmatic Book Allocation Formula for Academic and Public Libraries with a Test for Its Effectiveness." *Library Resources and Technical Services* vol. 19, no. 4 (Fall 1975): 356–68.

> *Description*: "A procedure is described for allocating based on (1) the premise that a library's collection should reflect the purpose of the institution, whether academic or public, and (2) the demand of the users as indicated by the number of books used and average cost of a book in given categories. For academic libraries, the subjects represented by departments provide a good framework for data collection. The subjects, as described by the departments themselves in the university bulletin, can in turn be described by Dewey or LC classification numbers. For public libraries, or for academic libraries not wishing to allocate to academic departments, the divisions of the Dewey or LC classification are sufficient. Two variables, the number of books circulated and the average cost of books in each category, are the essential ingredients of the allocation formula. The number of books circulated is multiplied by the average cost, and the product converted to a percentage of the overall cost-use. This percentage is the basic allocation value for the particular category, and is multiplied by the total dollar amount available for all categories.

> "A simple test for the effectiveness of allocation is to correlate current buying, or the distribution of books in the shelf list, with the distribution of circulation, using any nonparametric correlation statistic, such as Spearman's rank order statistic. If the correlations are high, the allocations are satisfactory ... If low, the procedure should be reexamined."

DILLEHAY MODEL

Dillehay, Bette. "Book Budget Allocation: Subject or Objective Approach." *Special Libraries* 62:509–14.

Abstract: "Budgetary control and financial management are keys to efficient utilization of resources invested in industrial libraries. While present methods of acquisition are geared to random selection of books based on user requests, such methods bear little relation to a balanced collection. A study was initiated to determine if an objective approach to budget allocation should be developed. Previous acquisitions were correlated with book circulation, books published, book costs and total research budget. The results indicate that acquisitions based on user requirements combined with a computer analysis of existing holdings produce a collection most valuable to the user community."

GOLD MODEL

Gold, Steven D. "Allocating the Book Budget: An Economic Model." *College and Research Libraries* Sept. 1975, p. 397–402.

Abstract: "A model is presented in which the division of library resources among competing interests is based upon considerations of economic efficiency. The complete model cannot be made operational until better means are developed to measure library-resource units. It is argued that allocation decisions should depend upon the prospective usage rate of materials, explicit value judgments about how much such use contributes to the university's goals, and costs."

KOHUT MODEL (1)

Kohut, Joseph J. "Allocating the Book Budget: A Model." *College and Research Libraries* May 1974, p. 192–99.

Abstract: Inflation is currently affecting library book budgets, particularly with respect to the acquisition of serials. A model is proposed which would balance the purchase of serials against the purchase of monographs by individual funding units within the academic library. Special consideration is given to inflation as a cost factor affected by both the form of the publication and the subject matter. Applying the model to a specific example demonstrated its use in providing control over collection development and allowing for equitable distribution of book funds among funding units."

From Conclusion: "Through appropriate inflation corrections ... it provides a mechanism for equitable distribution of book budget funds. An ancillary benefit is that it clearly maps the general direction in which the collection is developing and allows better control over collection development. The model is ... flexible in that it can incorporate any number of funding units (e.g., physics, English) and subdivisions thereof (e.g., periodicals, monographs)."

KOHUT MODEL (2)

Kohut, Joseph J., and Walker, John F. "Allocating the Book Budget: Equity and Economic Efficiency." *College and Research Libraries* Sept. 1975, p. 403–10.

Abstract: "Gold's cost-benefit model for allocating the book budget is critiqued from the point of view of practicability, economic theory, and equity. It is concluded that allocative formulas are preferred alternatives for distributing the book budget among departmental funds. Economic efficiency via cost-effectiveness analysis is suggested as potentially useful for within-fund acquisitions of library-resource units."

PIERCE MODEL

Pierce, Thomas John. "Economics of Library Acquisitions: A Book Budget Allocation Model for University Libraries." Ph.D. dissertation, University of Notre Dame, 1976.

Abstract: Pierce attempts to develop a framework for efficient and equitable distribution of book funds to academic departments of a university, based on the amount of relative departmental use of the library's collection and the department's average price of literature in its field. Using mathematical and statistical methods, Pierce derived a budget allocation model. It is recognized that the formula has limitations but that it is useful when applied along with a set of objective initial allotment figures based on library need.

Bibliographies

COLLECTION DEVELOPMENT POLICIES

American Library Association. Office of Intellectual Freedom. *Intellectual Freedom Manual*. Chicago: the Association, 1974.

Essential as back-up for a materials selection policy, this will also prove useful in developing the policy itself. "Development of a Materials Selection Program" (Part 4, pp. 5–10) covers the basic background information needed to develop a policy and outlines ideal content.

_____. Resources and Technical Services Division. Resources Section. Collection Development Committee. "Guidelines for the Formation of Collection Development Policies." *Library Resources and Technical Services* 21:40–47 (Winter 1977).

In an attempt to encourage some sort of standardization among collection development policies, ALA has provided this general statement outlining the essential components of such policies. Language codes and definitions of collection levels are included, as well as a minimum breakdown of LC classes suitable for the analysis of a collection by subject field.

Association of Research Libraries. Office of University Library Management Studies. Systems and Procedures Exchange Center. *Acquisition Policies in ARL Libraries*. Washington: ARL, 1974. Various paginations.

The brief introduction makes general statements about the function, characteristics, and development of collection development/acquisitions policies and reports some of the results of a SPEC collection development survey. These results relate to the frequency with which certain groups (director, reference librarians, faculty, etc.) participate in the formulation of the policies and the uses made of such policies (in order of importance). Eleven documents are included from various universities: comprehensive policy statements, short

58

general collection policy statements, statements for specific collections, cooperative arrangements for collection development, and the outline of a "mass
buying program."

————. ————. ————. *Collection Development in ARL Libraries.* Washington:
ARL, 1974. Various paginations.

Reports the results of a survey of 60 libraries regarding the organization of
the collection development function, including person or persons responsible,
degree of formal organization, role in the budget allocation process, presence
of a stated or unwritten policy. A copy of the questionnaire is included as well
as various types of documentation related to the organization of the collection
development function and the role of collection development committees. Six
institutions have provided position descriptions for collection development
officers.

————. ————. ————. *SPEC Kit 38: Collection Development Policies.* Washington:
ARL, 1977.

Baughman, James C. "Toward a Structural Approach to Collection Development." *College and Research Libraries* 38:241–48 (May 1977).

Boyer, Calvin J., and Eaton, Nancy L., eds. *Book Selection Policies in American
Libraries: an Anthology of Policies from College, Public and School Libraries.*
Austin, Texas: Armadillo Pr., 1971.

Basic content of a good selection policy is outlined in the introduction; text
of policy statements of ten colleges, fourteen public libraries, and seven school
systems are presented. Appendixes include various censorship-related statements.

Carter, Harriet H., and Palmer, Raymond A. "The Operation of a Rational
Acquisitions Committee." *Bulletin of the Medical Library Association* 65:
61–63 (January 1977).

The Miami Valley Association of Health Sciences Libraries established a
Rational Acquisitions Committee whose major objective has been to develop
guidelines for the cooperative purchasing of books and periodicals by the health
sciences libraries in the Dayton area. Subject areas were decided on and journals
assigned to particular groups. The text of the policy statement formulated by
the committee is given. The committee has also coordinated the addition and
withdrawal of books and periodical subscriptions within the member libraries.
To obtain a basis upon which to evaluate the importance of particular information resources, the committee sends an annual questionnaire to each member
requesting details of all journal citations borrowed from outside the local community in the previous year. This is used for recommending new subscriptions.

Carter, Mary Duncan, et al. *Building Library Collections.* 4th ed. Metuchen,
N.J.: Scarecrow, 1974.

Good background reading for principles governing good materials selection policies; variations based on type of library are discussed.

Coleman, Kathleen, and Dickinson, Pauline. "Drafting a Reference Collection Policy." *College and Research Libraries* 38:227–33 (May 1977).

A useful example of a collection development statement specifically for a reference collection. Brief introduction notes the uses for such policies, elements to be included, and the method used in drafting this particular policy. The collection for which the policy was designed (at San Diego State) is primarily social science and humanities, but the statement offers a useful model.

Converse, W. R. M., and Standers, O. R. "Rationalizing the Collections Policy: A Computerized Approach." Calgary: Calgary University Library, 1975. ERIC Document (ED 105 861).

An alternative to the traditional collection development statement, devised because the latter was viewed as insufficiently flexible and unresponsive to rapid change. Calgary has attempted "to incorporate the traditional collections policy statement in a management information system" which would permit updating at will. In addition to a file of collection development parameters for various departments, the data base includes a file of personnel which details each person's background as applicable to subject expertise.

De Vore, Helen L. "Acquisition Policy." *Special Libraries* 61:381–84 (Sept. 1970).

A policy to insure acquisition of primary international libraries; collections for a library system pertaining to the environmental sciences was prepared by a newly formed Technical Processes Section, ESSA. The policy was developed to be useful not only to operating personnel, but also to others on the staff of the ESSA Library System, to clientele, and to managers of the parent organization. Although the statement was prepared for a particular situation in federal libraries, it can be applied to other types of libraries.

Enoch Pratt Free Library, Baltimore. *How Baltimore Chooses; Selection Policies of the Enoch Pratt Free Library.* 4th ed. Baltimore: the Library, 1968.

A sample public library selection policy; considered one of the best.

Futas, Elizabeth, ed. *Library Acquisition Policies and Procedures.* Phoenix: Oryx Pr., 1977.

Selections from responses to a 1976 survey make up this book, containing 12 public library and 14 academic library policy statements representing libraries of various sizes, locations, and content. Also included are 56 partial selections from policies representing 18 public and 38 academic libraries. Appendixes include various official statements valuable as support documents.

Gaver, Mary Virginia, comp. *Background Readings in Building Library Collections.* 2 vols. Metuchen, N. J.: Scarecrow, 1969.

Section 2, "Development of a Selection Policy," provides a variety of points of view and types of library orientations, plus some sample policy statements.

Gratter, Mary C. "Collection Development in Texas State Agency Libraries; A Survey with Recommendations." *Special Libraries* 68:69–75 (Feb. 1977).

The second half of the article considers the need for state agency libraries to adopt a collection development policy, bearing in mind their problems with regard to increasing lack of space, limited budgets, and few staff. The core issue is public accountability—the public has a right to expect a collection to be kept in a condition allowing maximum use. Guidelines for the preparation of a written statement on collection development policy are presented under the following headings: Statement of purpose; Place of the librarian in the selection process; General criteria; Specific policies regarding special categories of materials; Unsolicited materials; Discard policies; Revision of collection development policy. Contains tables and a bibliography. For an abstract of the first half of the article, see entry at classification number Fju.

"Guidelines for Branch Libraries in Colleges and Universities." *College and Research Libraries News,* no. 9 (Oct. 1975), pp. 281–83.

"Guidelines for Two-Year College Learning Resources Programs." *College and Research Libraries News,* no. 11 (Dec. 1972), pp. 305–15.

Grube, Henner. "Methodological Problems in the Formulation of an Acquisitions Policy for a Public Library in the German Federal Republic; Die Estellung eines Erwerbungsplans fur eine Offentliche Bibliothek in der Bundesrepublik Deutschland: Methodische Probleme." *DFW Dokumentation-Information* 25:79–97 (May/June 1977).

In West Germany more discussion is needed on basic principles for the formulation of acquisitions policies. A preliminary outline should be made, setting out requisite tasks to be covered by the policy; detailed planning comes later. The planning process should be structured and the decision made as to who carries out the planning. Problems must be analyzed.

Klotzbucher, A. "The Changing Function of the University Library and Its Effect on the Acquisitions Policy." *Libri* 20:187–205 (1970).

Locker, Bernard. "Expediting Acquisitions of Government Documents." *Special Libraries* 62:9–16 (Jan. 1971).

U.S. Government documents rank among the most critically important publications acquired by special libraries. This paper outlines some practical guidelines as to what libraries can do to avoid pitfalls in their acquisition of government documents.

Lunsford, Effie B., and Kopkin, Theodore I. *A Basic Collection for Scientific and Technical Libraries.* New York: Special Libraries Association, 1971.

This list of selected technical literature was prepared as a guide for community colleges, technical institutes, and vocational schools in developing new libraries or enlarging existing collections. It was compiled by librarians of technical institutes in cooperation with faculty members of the Southern Technical Institute in Marietta, Georgia, and sponsored by the Special Libraries Association. Although the bibliography consists primarily of basic and standard books, and periodicals on the engineering technician level, it also contains some titles at other levels. Older and out-of-print editions have been included to serve as a guide in sorting gift collections and to indicate which titles may be used until they can be replaced with later editions. All books are in English.

Merritt, LeRoy Charles. *Book Selection and Intellectual Freedom.* Bronx, N. Y.: H. W. Wilson, 1970.

A useful, public library-oriented book containing three—adult, young adult, and children—composite selection policies derived from a large number of existing public library statements. Chapter 4, "Evaluating the Policy," discusses a variety of methods.

Opello, Olivia, and Murdock, Lindsay. "Acquisitions Overkill in Science Collections and an Alternative." *College and Research Libraries* 37:452–56 (Sept. 1976).

Librarians' solutions to space problems have centered around weeding and storage techniques. This article suggests that librarians should analyze their goals and acquisitions policies and redetermine their selection criteria. Discussed are the use made of library collections and reliance on circulation records as indicators of use; the cost of science books; scientists' information needs, which tend to focus on journal literature. The article concludes that science libraries often buy many unneeded books since these are the least-used source of information for physicists and other scientists. Therefore, highly selective and objective criteria need to be applied to book selection. Science libraries should concentrate on current awareness and information retrieval services based on the use of on-line systems and traditional abstracting and indexing services.

Osburn, Charles B. "Planning for a University Policy on Collection Development." *International Library Review* 9:209–24 (April 1977).

A summary of suggested considerations for the design of a comprehensive policy document for collection development. With the identification of purpose and attributes, looks at the substance of the document, the organization of substantive parts, and special features designed to facilitate interpretation. The policy document should be the product of maximum consultation at all stages of its development, with librarians and scholars as well as with those directly involved in the actual policy writing. Outlines a six-stage work plan for the drafting of a collection development policy.

Rice, Barbara A. "Development of Working Collections in University Libraries." *College and Research Libraries* 38:309–12 (July 1977).

Discusses in general terms how the scope of a collection should be defined and what types of specifications would appear in a collection development statement. A discussion of who should be responsible for the drafting of such statements stresses the importance of involving interested groups outside the library itself in the process; in addition, certain "publicity" functions which result from the formulation of these policies are noted. Implications for weeding, storage, exchange, etc. are touched upon.

Roper, Fred W. "Selecting Federal Publications." *Special Libraries* 65:326–31 (Aug. 1974).

The librarian who has the responsibility for adding federal documents to the collection is given some suggestions for selecting in both depository and non-depository libraries. Considerations for developing a selection policy for documents are discussed. Tools which may be of assistance for both retrospective and current documents are indicated.

Schwartz, James H. "Technical Books: Appraisal of Selection Policy and Use by Creative Chemists." *Special Libraries* 62:56–60 (Feb. 1974).

The effectiveness of a previously described ["Accessibility, Browsing, and a Systematic Approach to Acquisitions . . . ," *Special Libraries* 62:143–46 (March 1971)] acquisitions programs is discussed here along with user characteristics which verify the correlations between reading behavior and creativity.

Spiller, David. *Book Selection: An Introduction to Principles and Practice.* 2d ed. rev. Hamden, Conn.: Linnet Books and Clive Bingley, 1971.

This book covers all aspects of book selection and the factors that affect the budget goals, censorship, use and demand, internal systems of selection, book trade, and library supplier's cooperation.

"Standards for College Libraries." *College and Research Libraries News,* no. 9: 277–301 (Oct. 1975).

"Standards for Special Libraries." *Library Trends* 21:249–60 (Oct. 1972).

"Standards for University Libraries" (draft). *College and Research Libraries News,* no. 4:89–99 (April 1978).

"Standards in University Libraries." *Libri* 20:144–55 (1970).

Strauss, Lucille J.; Shreve, Irene M.; and Brown, Alberta L. *Scientific and Technical Libraries: Their Organization and Administration.* 2d ed. New York: Becker and Hayes, 1972.

This book provides an introduction to the organizational procedures and essential functions of a special library or information service in the sciences and their related technologies. It is primarily a guide to practices evolving from past experiences and recent developments. Chapter 5 covers selection and acquisition of books and other publications. Chapter 6 covers the selection, acquisition, and recording of periodicals.

Urguhart, D. J. "University Libraries: The Case for a National Lending System."
  Times Higher Education Supplement 256:8 (Sept. 1976).

The concept of the comprehensive university library collection still exists,
but the evidence is that libraries are not required to meet all user needs from
stock. Comprehensiveness is made unnecessary by bibliographies; the aim should
be to build effective collections of bibliographies in all subjects and provide
instruction for their proper use. The need is apparent for coordinating academic
library service, particularly where institutions are adjacent and better use must
be made of the British Library Lending Division. Public libraries make a big contribution to academic activities and the possibility of a national library system
cannot be ignored for long.

Ward, K. L. "Collection Policy in College and University Libraries." *Notes*
  (Music Library Association) 29:432–40 (March 1973).

Windsor, Donald A. "De-acquisitioning Journals Using Productivity/Cost Rankings." *De-acquisitions Librarian* 1:1, 8–10 (Spring 1976).

Faced with budget cuts in the area of journal acquisitions, the only recourse
is to make such cuts so that the loss to the library and the effect on service to
users will be minimized. One way of doing this is to rank the library's journals
to see which ones contribute the most articles within specific bibliographic ranges,
taking into account the cost of these articles in terms of annual subscription
costs. However, strict adherence to simple productivity rankings will produce a
false reading. To avoid this, the rank/cost factor of each journal must be calcu-
lated. Details of the method used to do this are provided. Obvious core journals
are exempted. An actual case study is given, showing the practical implementation of this method. Although arguments against ranking journals by article
productivity are legion, librarians will have to make some measurement decisions
if they are to come to terms with budget cuts and still serve their users.

Wise, Donald A. "Cartographic Sources and Procurement Problems." *Special
  Libraries* 68:198–205 (May/June 1977).

Various sources of cartographic materials are discussed. In addition, some
problems related to the procurement of these materials are investigated.

Wood, D. N. "Local Acquisition and Discarding Policies in the Light of National
  Library Resources and Services." *Aslib Proceedings* 29:24–34 (Jan. 1977).

Paper presented at the 50th Aslib Annual Conference, University of Exeter,
September 1976. Considers acquisition and discarding as two areas offering
scope for rationalization and cooperation between the British Library Lending
Division (BLLD) and local libraries. With regard to acquisition, the librarian
must predict demand and then compare the cost of buying, processing and
storing an item with the cost of obtaining it on interlibrary loan whenever it

is required. Some strategies for rationalizing journal acquisitions are summarized. A number of studies making suggestions on discard policies are reviewed, including the Atkinson report and research at Newcastle University. The findings of the Newcastle study are summarized in an appendix. Concludes with some comments on problems which might cause a deterioration in BLLD services: budgetary constraints, poor postal services, and the copyright question.

Wynar, Bohdan S. *Library Acquisitions: A Classified Bibliographic Guide to the Literature and Reference Tools.* Rochester, N.Y.: Libraries Unlimited, 1968.

The purpose of this work is to provide order librarians, and those responsible for the organization and administration of acquisition departments, with a comprehensive bibliographic guide to standard practices as expressed in the literature, and to list selected reference tools for various aspects of order work and book selection. The articles and books listed cover problems of acquisition work in all types of libraries: university, college, school, public, and special.

Yavarkovsky, J.; Mount, E.; and Kordish, H. "Computer-based Collection Development Statements for a University Library." *Proceedings of the 36th Annual Meeting of the American Society for Information Science, Los Angeles, October 21–25, 1973.* Vol. 10, Innovative Developments in Information Systems: Their Benefits and Costs. Edited by Helen J. Waldron and F. Raymond Long. Washington, D.C.: ASIS; Westport, Conn.: Greenwood Pr., 1973.

COLLECTION EVALUATION

Annotated Bibliographies

Bonn, George S. "Evaluation of the Collection." *Library Trends* 22:265–304 (1974).

A fundamental and useful annotated bibliography, despite a tendency to lose sight of the forest for the trees. Be sure to read the last pages (293 ff.) first.

Ifidon, Sam E. "Qualitative/Quantitative Evaluation of Academic Library Collections: A Literature Survey." *International Library Review* 8:299–308 (1976).

Critical summaries of nineteen articles and books; the focus is on optimal library size.

Lancaster, F. Wilfred. *The Measurement and Evaluation of Library Services.* Washington: Information Resources Pr., 1977.

The ultimate object of the chapter (pp. 165–206) on evaluation of the collection is to examine measures of collection use with the object of "optimizing storage of the collection." It remains a useful study with a substantial recent bibliography.

Otterson, Signe. "A Bibliography on Standards for Evaluating Libraries." *College and Research Libraries* 32:128–41 (1971).

Surveys

Hirsch, Rudolf. "Evaluation of Book Collections." *Library Evaluation.* Edited by Wayne S. Yenawine. Syracuse: Syracuse Univ. Pr., 1959.
Williams, Edwin E. "Surveying Library Collections." *Library Surveys.* Edited by Maurice F. Tauber and Irlene Roemer Stephens. Conference on Library Surveys, Columbia University, 1965. New York: Columbia Univ. Pr., 1967.

General

ACRL Committee on Liaison with Accrediting Agencies. "Guide to Methods of Library Evaluation." *College and Research Libraries News* 9:293–99 (1968). "An aid in judging the adequacy of an academic library."
Bach, Harry. "Acquisition Policy in the American Library." *College and Research Libraries* 18:441–51 (1957).
———. "Evaluation of the University Library Collection." *Library Resources and Technical Services* 2:24–29 (1958).
    Contains good bibliography of previous work on *surveying* library collections.
Baughman, James C. "Toward a Structural Approach to Collection Development." *College and Research Libraries* 38:241–48 (1977).
Bonn, George S. "Library Self-Surveys." *Library and Information Science* 9: 115–21 (1971).
McGrath, William E. "The Significance of Books Used According to a Classified Profile of Academic Departments." *College and Research Libraries* 33: 212–19 (1972).
Pennsylvania University. Library. *Changing Patterns of Scholarship and the Future of Research Libraries: A Symposium in Celebration of the 200th Anniversary of the Establishment of the University of Pennsylvania Library.* Edited by Rudolf Hirsch. Philadelphia: Univ. of Pennsylvania Pr., 1951.
Raney, M. Llewellyn. *The University Libraries.* Survey no. 7. Chicago: Univ. of Chicago Pr., 1933.
    The most evaluative of the early library collection surveys—a great pioneer study.
Stieg, Lewis. "A Technique for Evaluating the College Library Book Collection." *Library Quarterly* 12:34–44 (1943).
    An unfortunately disappointing essay on college collection evaluation.
Swank, Raynard C. "Too Much and Too Little: Observations on the Current

Status of Library Resources." *Library Resources and Technical Services* 3: 20–31 (1959).

Waples, Douglas, and Lasswell, Harold D. *National Libraries and Foreign Scholarship.* Chicago: Univ. of Chicago Pr., 1936.
Demonstrates superiority of subject specialists in building research library collections. (See also Danton, *Book Selection and Collections* below.)

Evaluation Reports — Academic Libraries

Burns, Robert W. *Evaluation of the Holdings in Science/Technology in the University of Idaho Library.* Univ. of Idaho Library Publication Number Two. Moscow: The Library, 1968.

Cassata, Mary B., and Dewey, Gene L. "The Evaluation of a University Library Collection: Some Guidelines." *Library Resources and Technical Services* 13:450–57 (1969).
Study of collection evaluations carried out at SUNY-Buffalo.

Golden, Barbara. "A Method for Quantitatively Evaluating a University Library Collection." *Library Resources and Technical Services* 18:268–74 (1974).
Quantitative evaluation of the University of Nebraska, Omaha, collections.

Tauber, Maurice F. "The Faculty and the Development of Library Collections." *Journal of Higher Education* 32:454–58 (1961).
Report on a collection evaluation at Columbia University.

University of Michigan. Survey Research Center. *Faculty Appraisal of a University Library by the Survey Research Center of the University of Michigan.* Ann Arbor: Univ. Library, 1961.

Webb, William. "Project Co Ed: a University Library Collection Evaluation and Development Program." *Library Resources and Technical Services* 13:457–62 (1969).
A very important study, useful for method.

Evaluation Report — Special Libraries

Coale, R. P. "Evaluation of a Research Library Collection: Latin-American Colonial History at the Newberry." *Library Quarterly* 35:173–84 (1965).

Miscellaneous Topics
Citation analysis

Singleton, Alan. "Journal Ranking and Selection: A Review in Physics." *Journal of Documentation* 32:258–86 (1976).
Suggestive critique of the significance and uses of citation analysis.

Collection quality

Danton, J. Periam. *Book Selection and Collections: A Comparison of German and American University Libraries.* New York and London: Columbia Univ. Pr., 1963.

A classic on quality in collection development; the subject is research libraries. Danton's range is broad, many of his views remain highly influential. A scholarly study of substance and depth.

Gormley, Mark M. "Academic Libraries." *Library Surveys.* Edited by Maurice F. Tauber and Irlene Roemer Stephens. Conference on Library Surveys, Columbia University, 1965. New York and London: Columbia Univ. Pr., 1967.

Evaluation for accreditation

Waples, Douglas. *The Evaluation of Higher Institutions IV. The Library.* Chicago: Univ. of Chicago Pr., 1937.

Formulas

McInnis, R. Marvin. "The Formula Approach to Library Size: An Empirical Study of Its Efficacy in Evaluating Research Libraries." *College and Research Libraries* 33:190–98 (1972).

Morse, Philip M. "Measures of Library Effectiveness." *Library Quarterly* 42: 15–30 (1972).

Library Needs of Scholars

Bestor, Arthur E. "The Transformation of American Scholarship, 1875–1917." *Library Quarterly* 23:173 (1953).

Library Survey Reports

Coney, Donald. *Report of a Survey of the Indiana University Library for the Indiana University, February-July, 1940.* Chicago: American Library Assn., 1940.

Downs, Robert B. *Resources of Canadian Academic and Research Libraries.* Ottawa: Association of Universities and Colleges of Canada, 1967.

Application of quantified standards to ascertain Canadian Research Library adequacy.

_____. *Union Catalogs in the United States.* Chicago: American Library Assn., 1942.

Chapter 4 is an attempt to measure adequacy of research library collections in the U.S.

Line, Maurice B. *Library Surveys: An Introduction to Their Use, Planning, Procedure and Presentation.* Hamden: Archon Books, 1967.

The standard English treatment. A handbook for surveying libraries. Includes some information on public library evaluation.

Potter, Alfred C. *The Library of Harvard University: Descriptive and Historical Notes.* Library of Harvard University, Special Publication, 6. Cambridge: Harvard Univ. Pr., 1934.

Wilson, Louis R., and Swank, Raynard C. *Survey of the Library of Stanford University, November, 1946 - March 1947.* Chicago: American Library Assn., 1947.

Individual Institutions

Bibliographical Planning Committee of Philadelphia. *A Faculty Survey of the University of Pennsylvania Libraries.* Philadelphia Library Resources, I. Philadelphia: Univ. of Pennsylvania Pr., 1940.

McCarthy, Stephen Anthony. *Report of a Survey of the Library of the University of New Hampshire, January-February 1949.* Durham: Univ. of New Hampshire Library, 1949.

Orr, Robert W., and Carlson, William H. *Report of a Survey of the Library of Texas A & M College, Oct., 1949 - Feb., 1950.* College Station: The Library, 1950.

Wilson, Louis R. *Report of a Survey of the Libraries of Cornell University, October, 1947 - February, 1948.* Ithaca: Cornell Univ. Pr., 1948.

Wilson, Louis R., and Orr, Robert W. *Report of a Survey of the Libraries of the Alabama Polytechnic Institute, Nov., 1948 - Mar., 1949.* Auburn, Alabama: The Institute, 1949.

Obsolescence

Line, Maurice B., and Sandison, A. " 'Obsolescence' and Changes in Use of Literature with Time." *Journal of Documentation* 30:283–350 (1974).

An important critique of obsolescence studies with bibliography and citation frequency lists.

Public Libraries

Chandler, George. "Objectives, Standards and Performance Measures for Metropolitan City Library Systems." *International Library Review* 2:457 (1970).

Quantification

California. University. Library. *Titles Classified by the Library of Congress*

Classification: Seventeen University Libraries. Preliminary ed. Edited by Le Roy D. Ortopan. Berkeley: General Library, 1973.

Ettlinger, John R. T. "Nation-wide Rationalization of Acquisition Policies in Canadian College and University Libraries: Are Total World Coverage and Non-duplication of Resources an Impossible Dream?" *Three papers on collections delivered at the Canadian Association of College and University Libraries Workshop on Collections Development held at Sackville, New Brunswick, June 17, 1973.* Halifax: Dalhousie University School of Library Service, 1975. Antiquantification.

_____. "Through a Glass Darkly—Academic Book Selection in Crisis." *Atlantic Province Library Association Bulletin* 33 (1969). Antiquantification.

Krikelas, James. "Library Statistics and the Measurement of Library Service." *ALA Bulletin,* 60:494–98 (1966). A helpful critique of the use of statistics in evaluating library services.

Miller, John. "The Problem of Fall-out from the Knowledge Explosion." *Atlantic Province Library Association Bulletin* 4:21–27 (1969). Antiquantification.

Piternik, George. "Library Growth and Academic Quality." *College and Research Libraries* 24:223–29 (1963). A suggestive critique of correlation between library growth rate and collection quality. Also a sound critique of the "Rider theory" and Axford's study thereof.

Use Studies

Simmons, Peter. *"Collection Development and the Computer: A Case Study in the Analysis of Machine Readable Loan Records and Their Application to Selection.* Vancouver: Univ. of British Columbia, 1971.

REVIEW OF LIBRARY COLLECTIONS

Weeding — General

Boyer, Calvin J., and Eaton, Nancy L. *Book Selection Policies in American Libraries: An Anthology of Policies from Colleges, Public and School Libraries.* Austin, Texas: Armadillo Pr., 1971.

Buckland, Michael K. *Book Availability and the Library User.* New York: Pergamon, 1975.

Buckland, Michael K., et al. *Systems Analysis of a University Library.* Occasional Papers, No. 4. Lancaster: Univ. of Lancaster Library, 1970.

Cooper, Marianne. "Cost of Weeding a Library Collection." *Library Journal* 91:194 (Jan. 15, 1966).

———. "Criteria for Weeding of Collections." *Library Resources and Technical Services* 12:339–51 (Summer 1968).

Erlich, Martin. "Do Not Discard." *Unabashed Librarian* 16:9–10 (Summer 1975).

Gore, Daniel, ed. *Farewell to Alexandria; Solutions to Space, Growth, and Performance Problems of Libraries.* Westport, Conn.: Greenwood Pr., 1976.

———. "View from the Tower of Babel." *Library Journal* 100:1599–1605 (Sept. 15, 1975); Comment (Letters) *Library Journal* 100:2081 (Nov. 15, 1975).

Leimkuhler, Ferdinand F., and Cooper, Michael David. "Analytical Models for Library Planning." *Journal of the American Society for Information Science* 22:390–98 (Nov. 1971).

MacDonald, Mary Beth. "Weeding the Collection." *Unabashed Librarian* 16:7–8 (Summer 1975).

McGaw, Howard F. "No Growth; When Is Not - Enough Enough? A Symposium." *Journal of Academic Librarianship* 1:4–11 (Nov. 1975).

———. "Policies and Practices in Discarding." *Library Trends* 4:269–82 (Jan. 1956).

Seymour, Carol A. "Weeding the Collection: A Review of Research on Identifying Obsolete Stock." *Libri* 22:137–48, 183–89 (1972).

"Stock Revision." In *Book Selection: An Introduction to Principles and Practice,* edited by David Spiller. 2d ed., rev. London: C. Bingley, 1974.

"Surveying and Weeding Collections; Surveying the Community." In *Building Library Collections,* edited by Mary Duncan Carter, et al. 4th ed. Metuchen, N. J.: Scarecrow Pr., 1974.

Trueswell, Richard W. "Determining the Optimal Number of Volumes for a Library's Core Collection." *Libri* 16:49–60 (1966).

———. "A Quantitative Measure of User Circulation Requirements and Its Possible Effect of Stock Thinning and Multiple Copy Determination." *American Documentation* 16:20–25 (Jan. 1965).

Windsor, Donald A. "De-Acquisitioning Journals Using Productivity/Cost Rankings," *De-Acquisitions Librarian Newsletter* 1:1, 8–10 (Spring 1976).

Woods, Donald A. "Weeding the Library Should Be Continuous." *Library Journal* 76:1193–96 (Aug. 1951).

Weeding — Academic Libraries

Andrews, Theodore A. "The Role of Departmental Libraries in Operations Research Studies in a University Library — Part I: Selection for Storage Problems." *Special Libraries* 59:519–24 (Sept. 1968).

Ash, Lee. "Comparison of Weeding Criteria: A Suboptimization." In *Systematic Analysis of University Libraries – An Application of Cost-Benefit Analysis to the M.I.T. Libraries,* edited by Jeffery A. Raffael and Robert A. Shisko. Cambridge: M.I.T. Pr., 1969.

_____. *Yale's Selective Book Retirement Program.* Hamden, Conn.: Anchor Books, 1963.

Farber, Evan Ira. "Limiting College Library Growth: Bane or Boon?" *Journal of Academic Librarianship* 1:12–15 (Nov. 1975).

Fussler, Herman H., and Simon, Julian L. *Patterns in the Use of Books in Large Research Libraries.* Chicago: Univ. of Chicago Library, 1969.

Gosnell, Charles F. "Obsolescence of Books in College Libraries." *College and Research Libraries* 5:115–25 (March 1944).

Grundt, Leonard. "Guidelines for Branch Libraries in College and Universities." *College and Research Libraries News,* pp. 281–83 (Oct. 1975).

_____. "Guidelines for Two-year College Learning Resources Programs." *College and Research Libraries News,* pp. 305–15 (Dec. 1972).

_____. "Nassau Community College Library Weeding Policy." *Unabashed Librarian* 16:12 (Summer 1975).

Rouse, Roscoe. "Within-library Solutions to Book Space Problems." *Library Trends* 19:299–310 (Jan. 1971).

Shipman, Joseph C. "Optimum Size and the Large Research Library." *College and Research Libraries* 27:354–57, 392 (Sept. 1966).

Simon, Julian L. "How Many Books Should Be Stored Where? An Economic Analysis." *College and Research Libraries* 28:92–103 (March 1967).

"Standards for College Libraries." *College and Research Libraries News* pp. 277–79, 290–95, 298–301 (Oct. 1975).

Thompson, James. "Revision of Stock in Academic Libraries." *Library Association Record* 75:41–44 (March 1973).

Totten, Herman L. "Selection of Library Material for Storage: A State of the Art." *Library Trends* 19:341–51 (Jan. 1971).

Weeding – Public Libraries

Bogart, Harold L. Weeding in the Public Library. Research Paper, State University of New York, Albany, 1973.

Castagna, Edwin. "Last Rites: Uneasy Business of Disposing of Bookish Remains." *AB Bookman's Weekly* 40:1191–94 (Oct. 2–9, 1967).

Erlich, Martin. "Pruning the Groves of Libraro: A Look at the Discard Dilemma." *Wilson Library Bulletin* 50:55–58 (Sept. 1975).

MacDonald, Mary Beth. "Weeding the Collection." *Library Development.* Victoria, B.C.: Library Development Commission, 1975.

Matthews, Miriam. "Improving the Book Collection: Quality through Weeding." *Oklahoma Librarian* 11:57–58 (Oct. 1961).

Murdoch, Mary E. "Improving the Book Collection: Weeding in Action." *Oklahoma Librarian* 11:79–81 (Oct. 1961).

Rush, Betsy. "Weeding vs. Censorship: Treading a Fine Line." *Library Journal* 99:3032–33 (Nov. 15, 1974).

Stoliarov, Iu. N. "Optimum Size of Public Library Stock." *UNESCO Bulletin for Libraries* 27:22–28, 42 (Jan./Feb. 1973).

Weeding — Special Libraries

Beatty, W. "Technical Processing: Part I, Selection, Acquisition, and Weeding." In *Handbook of Medical Library Practice*. Publication No. 4. Chicago: Medical Library Assn., 1970.

Bedsole, Danny T. "Formulating a Weeding Policy for Books in a Special Library." *Special Libraries* 49:205–9 (May/June 1958).

Martin, Jess A., and Manch, Steven B. "Library Weeds: Weeding Is Essential to the Efficient Operation of Medical Libraries." *Bulletin of the Medical Library Association* 59:599–602 (Oct. 1971).

Redmond, D. A. "Optimum Size: The Special Library Viewpoint." *SLA Sci-Tech News* 20:40–42 (Summer 1966).

Slote, Stanley, J. "An Approach to Weeding Criteria for Newspaper Libraries," *American Documentation,* 19:168–72 (April, 1968).

Storage

Ash, Lee M. *Yale's Selective Book Retirement Program*. Hamden: Anchor Books, 1963.

Buckland, Michael K. *Book Availability and the Library User*. New York: Pergamon, 1975.

Conger, Lucinda D. "Annex Library of Princeton University: The Development of a Compact Storage Library." *College and Research Libraries* 31:160–68 (May 1970).

Clapp, Verner W., and Jordan, Robert T. "Re-evaluation of Microfilm as a Method of Book Storage." *College and Research Libraries* 24:5–11 (Jan. 1963).

Cox, Julius. "Optimum Storage of Library Material." Ph.D. dissertation, Department of Industrial Engineering, Purdue University, 1964.

Ellsworth, Ralph E. *Buildings*. State of the Library Art, Vol. 3, pt. 1. New Brunswick, N.J.: Graduate School of Library Service, Rutgers Univ., 1960.

____. *The Economics of Book Storage in College and University Libraries.* Washington: Association of Research Libraries, 1969.

Esterquist, Ralph Theodore. "Comments on the Article Shelving Books by Size." *ALA Bulletin* 51:437 (June 1957).

Friley, Charles E., and Orr, Robert W. "Decade of Book Storage at Iowa State College." *College and Research Libraries* 12:7–10 (Jan. 1951).

Fussler, Herman, and Simon, Julian L. *Patterns in the Use of Books in Large Research Libraries.* Chicago: Univ. of Chicago Library, 1969.

Gawrecki, Drahoslav. *Compact Library Shelving.* Translated by S. Rehak. Chicago: ALA, Library Technology Program, 1968.

Gore, Daniel, ed. *Farewell to Alexandria, Solutions to Space, Growth, and Performance Problems of Libraries.* Westport, Conn.: Greenwood Pr., 1976.

Grieder, Elmer M. "The Effect of Book Storage on Circulation Service." *College and Research Libraries* 11:374–76 (Oct. 1959).

Gupta, Surendra Mohan, and Ravindran, Arunachalam. "Optimal Storage of Books by Size: An Operations Research Approach." *Journal of the American Society for Information Service* 25:354–57 (Nov. 1974). Comment by M. K. Buckland: *Journal of the American Society for Information Science* 26: 351–52 (Nov. 1975).

Harrar, Helen Joanne. "Cooperative Storage." *Library Trends* 19:318–28 (Jan. 1971).

____. "Cooperative Storage Warehouses." Ph.D. dissertation, Rutgers Univ., 1962.

Hill, Francis John. "Storage in University Library Buildings." *UNESCO Bulletin for Libraries* 17:337–45 (Nov. 1963).

Hopp, Ralph H. "Problems of Storing University Library Materials." *College and Research Libraries* 22:435–37 (Nov. 1961).

Humenuk, Stanley. *Automatic Shelving and Book Retrieval: A Contribution Toward a Progressive Philosophy of Library Service for a Research Library.* Occasional Papers, No. 78. Urbana: Graduate School of Library Service, Univ. of Illinois, 1976.

Lee, James D. "Book Storage as One Aspect of Cooperation." *Southeastern Librarian* 21:161–68 (Fall 1971).

Leimkuhler, Ferdinand F., and Cox, J. Grady. "Compact Book Storage in Libraries." *Operations Research* 12:414–27 (May/June 1964).

Lister, Winston Charles. "Least-Cost Decision Rules for the Selection of Library Materials for Compact Storage." Ph.D. dissertation, Purdue Univ. 1967. (NTIS Document No. PB 174 441.)

Metcalf, Keyes D. "Compact Shelving." *College and Research Libraries* 23:110 (March 1962).

————. "The New England Deposit Library after Thirteen Years." *Harvard Library Bulletin* 8:313–22 (1954).

————. *Planning Academic and Research Libraries.* New York: McGraw-Hill, 1965.

Muller, Robert Hans. "Economics of Compact Book Shelving." *Library Trends* 13:433–47 (April 1965).

————. "Toward a National Plan for Cooperative Storage and Retention of Little-Used Library Materials." In *Resource Sharing in Libraries,* edited by Allen Kent, pp. 119–28. New York: Marcel Dekker, 1974.

Orne, Jerrold. "Storage and Deposit Libraries." *College and Research Libraries* 21:446–52, 461 (Nov. 1960).

————. *Storage Warehouses.* State of the Library Art, Vol. 3, pt. 3. New Brunswick, N.J.: Graduate School of Library Science, Rutgers Univ., 1960.

Perrine, R. H. *Library Space Survey of Texas Colleges and Universities.* Austin: Coordinating Board, Texas Colleges and University System, 1970. Summary: "Toward Better Library Holdings in Texas." *Texas Libraries* 32:188–90 (Winter 1970).

Piternick, George. *Book Storage in Academic Libraries. A Report Submitted to the Council on Library Resources.* 1974. (ERIC Document ED 112 835.)

Redmond, D. A. "Optimum Size: The Special Library Viewpoint." *SLA Sci-Tech News* 20:40–42 (Summer 1966).

Rider, Fremont. *Compact Book Storage.* New York: Hadham Pr., 1949.

————. *The Scholar and the Future of the Research Library.* New York: Hadham Pr., 1944.

Roffel, L. J. "Compact Book Storage Models." Ph.D. dissertation, Purdue Univ., 1965.

Rogers, Rutherford D. "Shelving Books by Size." *ALA Bulletin,* 51:435–37 (June 1957).

Shipman, Joseph C. "Optimum Size and the Large Science Research Library." *College and Research Libraries* 27:354–57, 392 (Sept. 1966).

Simon, Julian. "How Many Books Should Be Stored Where? An Economic Analysis." *College and Research Libraries* 28:92–103 (March 1967).

Snowball, George J., and Sampedero, Joseph. "Selection of Periodicals for Return to Prime Space from a Storage Facility." *Canadian Library Journal* 30:490–92 (Nov. 1973).

"Storing the Collection." In *Systematic Analysis of University Libraries — An Application of Cost Benefit Analysis to the M.I.T. Libraries,* edited by Jeffrey A. Raffael and Robert A. Shisko, pp. 7–22. Cambridge: M.I.T. Pr., 1969.

Totten, Herman L. "Selection of Library Materials for Storage: A State of the Art." *Library Trends* 19:341–51 (Jan. 1971).

Book Use

Davis, Richard A., and Bailey, Catherine A. *Bibliography of Use Studies.* Philadelphia: Graduate School of Library Science, Drexel Institute of Technology, 1964.

Jain, Adridman K. "Sampling and Short-Period Usage in the Purdue Library." *College and Research Libraries* 27:211–18 (May 1966).

____. "A Statistical Study of Book Use Supplemented with a Bibliography of Library Use Studies." Ph.D. dissertation, Purdue Univ., 1967.

McGrath, William E. "Correlating the Subjects of Books Taken Out of and Books Used within an Open-Stack Library." *College and Research Libraries* 32:280–85 (July 1971).

Mueller, Elizabeth. "Are New Books Read More than Old Ones?" *Library Quarterly* 25:166–72 (July 1965).

Slote, Stanley James. "The Predictive Value of Past-Use Patterns of Adult Fiction in Public Libraries for Identifying Core Collections." Ph.D. dissertation, Rutgers Univ., 1970.

Trueswell, Richard W. *Analysis of Library User Circulation Requirements.* Amherst: Univ. of Massachusetts, 1968.

____. "Determining the Optimal Number of Volumes for a Library's Core Collection." *Libri* 16:49–60 (1966).

____. "A Quantitative Measure of User Circulation Requirements and Its Possible Effect on Stack Thinning and Multiple Copy Determination." *American Documentation* 16:20–25 (Jan. 1965).

____. "User Circulation Satisfaction vs. Size of Holdings at Three Academic Libraries." *College and Research Libraries* 30:204–13 (May 1969).

Obsolescence of Periodical Literature

Brookes, B. C. "Growth, Utility and Obsolescence of Scientific Periodical Literature." *Journal of Documentation* 26:283–94 (Sept. 1970).

____. "Obsolescence of Special Library Periodicals." *Journal of the American Society for Information Science* 21:320–29 (Sept. 1970).

Buckland, Michael Keeble. "Are Obsolescence and Scattering Related?" *Journal of Documentation* 28:242–46 (Sept. 1972).

Buckland, Michael Keeble, and Woodburn, S. *Some Implications for Library Management of Scattering and Obsolescence.* Library Occasional Papers, No. 1. Lancaster, England: Univ. of Lancaster, 1968.

Cole, P.F. "Journal Use Versus Age of Journal." *Journal of Documentation* 19:1–11 (March 1963).

Line, Maurice Bernard. "Half-Life of Periodical Literature: Apparent and Real Obsolescence." *Journal of Documentation* 26:53–54 (March 1970).

Ravichandra Rao, I. K. "Growth of Periodicals and Obsolescence of Articles in Periodicals: A Case Study in Sociology." *Library Science with a Slant to Documentation* (Bangalore, India), 11:92–96 (June 1974).

Sandison, A. "Use of Older Literature and Its Obsolescence." *Journal of Documentation* 27:184–99 (Sept. 1971).

Strain, Paula M. "A Study of the Usage and Retention of Technical Periodicals." *Library Resources and Technical Services* 10:295–304 (Summer 1966).

Citation Analysis

Garfield, Eugene. "Citation Analysis as a Tool in Journal Evaluation." *Science* 178:471–79 (Nov. 3, 1972).

Scales, Pauline A. "Citation Analysis as Indicators of the Use of Serials: A Comparison of Ranked Title Lists Produced by Citation Counting and from Use Data." *Journal of Documentation* 32:17–25 (March 1976).

ALLOCATION OF LIBRARY BOOK FUNDS

Allen, Kenneth S. *Current and Emerging Budgeting Techniques in Academic Libraries, Including a Critique of the Model Budget Analysis Program of the State of Washington.* Seattle: Univ. of Washington, 1972.

American Library Association. Association of College and Research Libraries. "Standards for College Libraries; Approved as Policy by the Board of Directors of the Association of College and Research Libraries, on July 3, 1975." *College and Research Libraries News* 9:277–79 (Oct. 1975).

Bach, Harry. "Why Allocate?" *Library Resources and Technical Services* 8: 161–65 (Spring 1964).

Clapp, Verner W., and Jordan, Robert T. "Quantitative Criteria for Adequacy of Academic Library Collections." *College and Research Libraries* 26:371–80 (Sept. 1965).

Dillehay, Bette. "Book Budget Allocation: Subjective or Objective Approach." *Special Libraries* 62:504–14 (Dec. 1971).

Gold, Steven D. "Allocating the Book Budget: an Economic Model." *College and Research Libraries* 36:397–402 (Sept. 1975).

Goyal, S. K. "Allocation of Library Funds to Different Departments of a University: an Operational Research Approach." *College and Research Libraries* 34:219–22 (May 1973).

Headings, Bernice E. "The Formulation of a Book Budget Policy for Small College Libraries." *Wilson Library Bulletin* 26:389–93 (Jan. 1952).

Kohut, Joseph J. "Allocating the Book Budget: a Model." *College and Research Libraries* 35:192–99 (May 1974).

Kohut, Joseph J., and Walker, John F. "Allocating the Book Budget: Equity and Economic Efficiency." *College and Research Libraries* 36:403–10 (Sept. 1975).

McGrath, William E. "An Allocation Formula Derived from a Factor Analysis of Academic Departments." *College and Research Libraries* 30:51–62 (Jan. 1969).

____. "A Pragmatic Book Allocation Formula for Academic and Public Libraries with a Test for Its Effectiveness." *Library Resources and Technical Services* 19:356–69 (Fall 1975).

Pierce, Thomas John. "The Economics of Library Acquisitions: a Book Budget Allocation Model for University Libraries." Ph.D. dissertation, Univ. of Notre Dame, 1976.

Schad, Jasper G. "Allocating Book Funds: Control of Planning?" *College and Research Libraries* 31:155–59 (May 1970).

Voigt, Melvin J. "Acquisition Rates in University Libraries." *College and Research Libraries* 36:263–71 (July 1975).